Catalogue of Ancient Coins in the Ossoliński National Institute Library

Part 2

Coins of the Roman Empire

Augustus – Domitianus

Polska Akademia Nauk
Zakład Narodowy im. Ossolińskich
Biblioteka

Katalog starożytnych monet w zbiorach Biblioteki Zakładu Narodowego im. Ossolińskich

Opracowała
Gabriela Sukiennik

Część 2

Monety Cesarstwa Rzymskiego. August – Domicjan

Polish Academy of Sciences
Ossoliński National Institute
Library

Catalogue of Ancient Coins in the Ossoliński National Institute Library

by
Gabriela Sukiennik

Part 2

Coins of the Roman Empire. Augustus – Domitianus

Wrocław · Warszawa · Kraków · Gdańsk · Łódź
Zakład Narodowy im. Ossolińskich
Wydawnictwo Polskiej Akademii Nauk
1989

Okładkę projektowała Anna Płotnicka

Fotografie wykonał Edmund Witecki

Pracę opiniował do druku Lesław Morawiecki

Redaktor Krzysztof Plater

Redaktor techniczny Anna Kowalska-Grygajtis

ISBN 83-04-02571-X

Zakład Narodowy im. Ossolińskich — Wydawnictwo.
Wrocław 1989.
Nakład: 780 egz.
Objętość: ark. wyd. 9,50; ark. druk. 6+3 (wkł.); ark. A_1 — 12.
Papier offset. kl. III, 80 g, 70 × 100.
Oddano do składania 1987. 06. 26.
Podpisano do druku 1989. 06. 12.
Druk ukończono we wrześniu 1989.
Wrocławska Drukarnia Naukowa. Zam. 3070/88.

Contents

Preface

After the catalogue of republican coins, published in 1986, now appears, as the second in the series, the present volume covering the coins of the Julian-Claudian and Flavian dynasties. It starts the presentation of the coins of the Roman Empire in Ossolineum collections. In this catalogue 493 coins from the years between 20 BC and AD 90 have been described. Besides coins traditionally held for imperial, provincial coins, both from the east and the west of the Empire, have been included. Up to now catalogues of imperial and provincial coins have been published separately, which made it rather difficult to evaluate properly the coinage of the Empire as a whole. The concentration of scientific attention on imperial and senate coins meant in practice undervaluation or perfunctory treatment of the economic role of the provinces. The joint presentation of these two currents of coinage, albeit incomplete, since there is no complete set of the provincial coins in the Ossolineum collection, is intended to constitute a step towards the reconstruction of a comprehensive picture of the Roman Empire coinage in time segments under emperors.

Also covered in the catalogue are untypical coins, the so-called hybrids, resulting from the combination of different pairs of dies of the obverse and the reverse. Moreover, included are descriptions of even very controversial coins which have usually been ignored in hitherto existing catalogues, namely fakes and imitations. No attempt has been made to determine the date or place of their creation. The metallic structure of the collection is as follows: there are 137 silver and 356 bronze coins in it. In their majority they have not been included in any hitherto published documentation. Only the Alexandrian coins have been presented in the form of a separate article. The collection derives from the old Ossolineum fonds, a fact that has been described in detail in the Foreword to the first part of the catalogue.

In cataloguing the coins included in the present volume the following collection catalogues have been taken into account: H. Mattingly, *Coins of the Roman Empire in the British Museum*, London 1930; C. H. V. Sutherland, C. M. Kraay, *Catalogue of Coins of the Roman Empire in the Asmolean Museum*, part 1 Augustus, Oxford 1975; J.-B. Giard, *Catalogue des monnaies de l'Empire Romain de la Bibliothèque Nationale*, vol. 1, Paris 1976; the catalogues of the types of imperial coins are: H. Mattingly, E. A. Sydenham, *The Roman Imperial Coinage*, vol. 1 and 2, London 1926 as well as the re-edition of the first volume made by C. H. V. Sutherland, in which he makes use of the results of the discussion that has been going on for a number of years on the beginnings of the Roman Empire coinage.

The arrangement adopted in the catalogue, as well as the datation and determination of types, is based on the above mentioned Sutherland's re-edition with regard to the period from Augustus to Nero. The description of the coins of Vespasian and his sons has been modelled on the first edition of the second volume of RIC. The present catalogue has the following arrangement: the coins have been classified under emperors, within these limits under metals they are made of, then chronologically and under issues. Detailed descriptions include all metrological data in grams and millimetres.

Translated by Lech Czyżewski

Wstęp

Po opublikowanym w 1985 r. katalogu monet republikańskich jako kolejny ukazuje się tom obejmujący monety dynastii julijsko-klaudyjskiej i flawijskiej. Rozpoczyna on prezentację monet Cesarstwa Rzymskiego w zbiorach Ossolineum. Opisano w nim 493 monety z lat od 20 p.n.e. do 90 r. Oprócz monet tradycyjnie uznanych za imperialne włączone do katalogu zostały monety prowincjonalne, zarówno z zachodu, jak i ze wschodu cesarstwa. Do tej pory katalogi monet imperialnych i prowincjonalnych publikowano oddzielnie, co w dużej mierze utrudniało właściwą ocenę mennictwa cesarstwa jako całości. Koncentrowanie uwagi badawczej na monetach cesarskich i senackich oznaczało w praktyce niedocenianie lub pobieżne traktowanie roli gospodarczo-ekonomicznej prowincji. Zestawienie w katalogu tych dwóch nurtów menniczych – choć niepełne, gdyż w kolekcji ossolińskiej nie ma kompletnego zasobu monet prowincjonalnych – stanowić ma w zamierzeniu krok w kierunku odtworzenia całościowego obrazu mennictwa imperium rzymskiego w odcinkach czasowych według panujących.

Umieszczono w katalogu także opisy monet nietypowych, tak zwanych hybryd, powstałych przez połączenie różnych par stempli awersu i rewersu. Włączone zostały ponadto opisy monet bardzo dyskusyjnych i w dotychczasowych katalogach w większości pomijanych, a mianowicie fałszerstwa i naśladownictwa. Przy monetach tych nie podjęto próby określenia czasu i miejsca powstania. Struktura kruszcowa zbioru przedstawia się następująco: monet srebrnych w zbiorze jest 137, brązowych 356. W większości są to monety nie objęte dokumentacją publikacyjną. Jedynie monety aleksandryjskie odnotowane zostały w formie osobnego artykułu. Zbiór pochodzi z dawnej kolekcji ossolińskiej, co szczegółowo przedstawiono w przedmowie do części pierwszej katalogu.

Przy opracowaniu monet włączonych do niniejszego tomu uwzględnione zostały następujące katalogi kolekcji: H. Mattingly: *Coins of the Roman Empire in the British Museum*, London 1930; C. H. V. Sutherland, C. M. Kraay: *Catalogue of Coins of the Roman Empire in the Asmolean Museum*, part 1 Augustus, Oxford 1975; J.-B. Giard: *Catalogue des monnaies de l'Empire Romain de la Bibliothèque Nationale*, vol. 1, Paris 1976; katalogi typów monet imperialnych to: H. Mattingly, E. A. Sydenham: *The Roman Imperial Coinage*, Vol. 1 i 2, London 1926, oraz reedycja tomu pierwszego dokonana przez C. H. V. Sutherlanda, w której wykorzystuje wyniki toczącej się od lat dyskusji nad początkami mennictwa cesarstwa rzymskiego.

Przyjęte w katalogu układ, datacja i określenie typów oparte są na tej właśnie reedycji Sutherlanda w odniesieniu do okresu od Augusta do Nerona.

Wzorem do opracowania monet Wespazjana i jego synów pozostało pierwsze wydanie tomu drugiego RIC. Katalog niniejszy ma następujący układ: monety podzielone zostały według poszczególnych panujących, w ich obrębie według metali, w których zostały wybite, następnie chronologicznie i według emisji. Szczegółowe opisy uwzględniają wszystkie dane metrologiczne w gramach i milimetrach.

Abbreviations

A — C. H. V. Sutherland, C. M. Kraay, *Catalogue of Coins of the Roman Empire in the Asmolean Museum*, Part 1 Augustus, Oxford 1975

A. G. — A. Geissen, *Katalog Alexandrinischer Kaisermünzen der Sammlung des Institut für Altertumskunde der Universität zu Köln*, Oplanden 1974. Bd 1. Augustus – Trajan

BMC — H. Mattingly, *Coins of the Roman Empire in the British Museum*, London 1930

BMC Alexsandria — R. S. Poole, *Catalogue of the Coins of Alexandria and the Nomes*, Bologna 1965

BMC Corinth — B. V. Head, *Catalogue of Greek Coins Corinth, Colonies of Corinth*, Bologna 1963

BMC Galatia, Cappadotia, Syria — W. Wroth, *Catalogue of the Greek Coins of Galatia, Cappadotia and Syria*, Bologna 1965

BMC Macedonia — B. V. Head, *Catalogue of Greek Coins Macedonia, etc.*, Bologna 1964

BMC Palestine — G. F. Hill, *Catalogue of the Greek Coins of Palestine*, Bologna 1965

BNC — J-B. Giard, *Catalogue des monnaies de l'Empire Romain de la Bibliothèque Nationale*, Vol. 1, Paris 1976

C. — H. Cohen, *Description Historique des Monnaies*, Paris 1955

RIC — H. Mattingly, E. A. Sydenham, *The Roman Imperial Coinage*, London 1926, Vol. 1 and 2

RICr — C. H. V Sutherland, *The Roman Imperial Coinage*, London 1984, Vol. 1, Revised Edition

Villaronga — L. Villaronga, *Numismatica antiqua de Hispania*, Barcelona 1979

Vives — A. Vives Escudero, *La moneda hispanica*, Madrid 1926

AE — Bronze

AR — Silver

As — As

D — Denarius

Dp — Dupondius

Orch — Orichalcum

Q — Quinarius

Quad — Quadrans

S — Sestertius

Tetrdr — Tetradrachma

There is an illustration of each coin.
The coins and their photographs have the same numbers.
Illegible letters are indicated in square brackets.

Catalogue

AUGUSTUS (27 B.C. – A.D. 14)

Imperial Issues

No.	Metal Size Weight	Axis	Deno-mina-tion	Obverse	Reverse
HISPANIA					
Mint of Colonia Patricia? c. 20–19 B.C.					
1	AR 19,4 3.570	↓	D	Head of Augustus, laureate, r.	CAESAR (above), AVGVSTVS (below); two laurel-branches.
c. 19 B.C.					
2	AR 17.6 3.670	↓	D	CAESAR [AVGVSTVS]. Head of Augustus, bare, r.	OB CIVIS SERVATOS in three lines in oak-wreath.
GALLIA					
Mint of Lugdunum 15–13 B.C.					
3	AR 18.0 3.360	↓	D	AVGVSTV[S] DIVI F; head of Augustus, bare, r.	IMP X; bull charging r.
8–7 B.C.					
4	AR 18.0 3.340	↓	D	AVGVSTVS DIVI F; head of Augustus, laureate, r.	C CAES [AVGVS] F; C. Caesar galloping r., holding reins in r. hand, in l. sword and shield; behind, eagle between two standards.

---

[1] RICr 51, RIC 268, BMC 318, A 39, BNC 1225.
[2] RICr 77a, RIC 290, BMC 378, A 58, BNC 1154
[3] RICr 167a, RIC 327, BMC 451, A 115, BNC 1373.
[4] RICr 199, RIC 348, BMC 500, A 150, BNC 1463.

No.	Metal Size Weight	Axis	Denomination	Obverse	Reverse
2 B.C.–A.D. 14					
5	AR 19.2 3.780	→	D	CAESAR AVGVS[TVS] DIVI F PATER [PATRIAE]; head of Augustus, laureate, r.	[C L] CAE[SARES] in ex. AVGVSTI F COS [DESIG] PRINC IVVENT. Caius and Lucius standing front, each togate and resting hand on shield; behind each shield, a spear; above, simpulum and lituus.
6	AR 19.1 3.795	↘	D	Similar, but CAESAR AVGVSTVS DIVI F PATER PATRIAE.	Similar, but [C L] CAE[SARES] AVGVSTI F COS DESIG PRINC IVVENT.
"Altar Series" 15 B.C.–10 B.C.					
7	AE 24.2 10.620	↑	As	CAESAR [PON MAX]; head of Augustus, laureate, r.	ROM ET AVG; front elevation of the Altar of Lugdunum, flanked by Victories.
8	AE 25.0 9.650	↘	As	Similar, but CAESAR PONT MAX. Countermark.	Similar.
Coins with Tiberius' name A.D. 12					
9	AE 26.4 12.660	↗	Dp	TI [CAES]AR AVGVST F IMPERAT VII; head of Tiberius, laureate, r.	ROM ET AVG; front elevation of the Altar of Lugdunum, lanked by Victories

ITALIA

Mint of Brundisium and Rome?
c. 32–29 B.C.

No.	Metal Size Weight	Axis	Denomination	Obverse	Reverse
10	AR 19.3 3.440	↘	D	Head of Venus r., wearing stephane and necklace.	C[CAESAR] – DIVI [F] to l. and r. of Octavian in military dress advancing l.; in l. hand spear. r. extended.

---

[5] RICr 297, RIC 350, BMC 519, A 156, BNC 1651.
[6] RICr 207, RIC 350, BMC 519, A 156, BNC 1651.
[7] RICr 230, RIC 360, BMC 549, A 337, BNC 1472.
[8] RICr 230, RIC 360, BMC 549, A 337, BNC 1472, countermark?
[9] RICr 244, RIC 370, BMC 583, A 385, BNC 1765.
[10] RICr 251, RIC 2, BMC 609, A 196, BNC 1.

No.	Metal Size Weight	Axis	Denomination	Obverse	Reverse
11	AR 19.3 3.430	↖	D	Head of Pax r., wearing stephane; behind, cornucopiae, in front, olivespray.	[C]AESAR DIVI F to l. and r. of Octavian standing r., r. hand raising, l. holding spear over shoulder.
12	AR 19.7 3.640	↘	D	Head of Octavian, bare, l.	CAESAR DIVI F to l. and r. Victory, standing on globe r., holding wreath in r. hand, in l. palm.
29–26 B.C.					
13	AR 12.8 1.725	↑	Q	[CAESAR] IMP VII; head of Octavian, bare, r.	[ASIA] RECEPTA; Victory standing l. on cista mystica between snakes. Victory holding wreath and palm.
Mint of Rome *Issues of Triumviri* 16 B.C.					
C. Asinius Gallus					
14	AE 31.7 21.875	↘	S	[OB] CIVIS SERVATOS in oak-wreath flanked by two laurel-branches.	C [ASINIVS] C F GALLVS III VIR A A A F F round S C.
15	AE 26.8 10.455	↘	As	CAESAR AVGVSTVS [TRI]BVNIC POTEST; head of Augustus, bare, r.	Similar, but C ASINIVS GALLVS [III VIR] A A A F F.
16	AE 26.3 10.100	←	As	Similar, but CAESAR AVGVSTVS [TRIBV]NIC POTEST.	Similar, but [C ASI]- NIVS GALLVS III VIR A A A F F.
15 B.C. L. Naevius Surdinus					
17	AE 27.2 9.950	↑	As	CAESAR AVGVSTVS [TRIBVNIC POT]EST; head of Augustus, bare, r.	L SVR[DINVS III VIR] A A A F F round S C.

[11] RICr 253, RIC 3, BMC 611, A 193, BNC 6.
[12] RICr 255, RIC 28, BMC 604, A 191, BNC 41.
[13] RICr 276, RIC 18, BMC 647, A 237, BNC 899.
[14] RICr 370, RIC 76, BMC 157, A 502, BNC 372.
[15] RICr 373, RIC 78, BMC 161, A 509, BNC 384.
[16] RICr 373, RIC 78, BMC 161, A 509, BNC 384.
[17] RICr 386, RIC 74, BMC 144, A 478, BNC 483.

No.	Metal Size Weight	Axis	Denomination	Obverse	Reverse
C. Plotius Rufus					
18	AE 27.0 8.825	←	As	CAESAR AV[GVSTVS TRIB]VNIC POT[EST]; head of Augustus, bare, r.	C PLO[TIVS RVFV]S III VIR A A A F F round S C.
9 B.C. Lamia, Silius, Annius					
19	AE 16.8 2.945	↘	Qd	LAMIA SILIVS ANNIVS; simpulum and lituus.	III VIR A A A F F round S C.
20	AE 15.8 3.355	↓	Qd	Similar, but [LAMIA SILIV]S ANNIVS.	Similar, but III VIR [A A] A F F.
21	AE 17.2 2.700	↖	Qd	Similar, but LAMIA SILIVS ANNIVS.	Similar, but III VIR A A [A F F].
22	AE 10.6 2.950	↗	Qd	[LAMIA] SILIVS ANN IVS; S – C to l. and r. cornucopiae.	III VIR A A A F F; altar.
23	AE 10.1 2.885	↑	Qd	Similar, but L[A]M[IA] [SIL]IVS ANNIVS.	I[II VIR] A A A F F; altar.
8 B.C. Pulcher, Taurus, Regulus					
24	AE 18.6 3.255	↘	Qd	PVLCHER TAVRVS REGVLVS; simpulum and lituus.	III VIR A A A F F round S C.
7. B.C. P. Lurius Agrippa					
25	AE 24.7 11.050	→	As	CAESAR AV[GUST PONT MAX TRIBVNIC POT]; head of Augustus, bare, r.	[P] LVRIVS AGRIPPA III VIR [A A A F F] round S C.

[18] RICr 389, RIC 69, BMC 153, A 491, BNC 503.
[19] RICr 421, RIC 181, BMC 201, A 561, BNC 580.
[20] RICr 421, RIC 181, BMC 201, A 561, BNC 580.
[21] RICr 421, RIC 181, BMC 201, A 561, BNC 580.
[22] RICr 422, RIC 182, BMC 202, A 565, BNC 589.
[23] RICr 422, RIC 182, BMC 202, A 565, BNC 589.
[24] RICr 424, RIC 184, BMC 205, A 572, BNC 606.
[25] RICr 427, RIC 186, BMC 209, A 576, BNC 621.

No.	Metal Size Weight	Axis	Denomination	Obverse	Reverse
26	AE 26.6 9.775	↘	As	Similar, but CAE[SAR AVGVST PONT MAX TRI]BVNIC PO[T].	Similar, but P LVRIVS A[G]RIPPA III VIR A A A F F.
27	AE 27.0 11.220	↑	As	Similar, but [CAESAR AVGVST PON]T MAX TRIBVNI[C POT].	Similar, but P LVRIVS AGRIPPA III VIR A A A F F.
M. Salvius Otho					
28	AE 25.5 10.275	↘	As	[CAESAR AVGVST PON]T MAX TRIBV[NIC POT]; head of Augustus, bare, r.	M SALV[IVS] OTHO [III VIR A] A A F F round S C.
29	AE 26.3 10.005	↑	As	Similar, but [CAESAR AVGVST] PONT MAX TRI[BVNIC POT].	Similar, but [M SA]LVIVS OTHO III VIR A A A [F F].
M. Maecilius Tullus					
30	AE 27.2 12.350	→	As	CAESAR AVGVST PONT [MAX TRIBVNIC POT]; head of Augustus, bare, r.	M MA[ECILIVS T] VLLVS III VIR A A A F F round S C.
31	AE 27.6 7.675	↑	As	Similar, but CAESAR [AVGVST P]ONT MAX TRIBV[NIC POT].	Similar, but [M MAESI]-LIVS TVLLVS III VIR A A A F F.
4 B.C. P. Betilienus Bassus					
32	AE 15.5 2.725	↗	Qd	[P] BETILIE[NVS] BASSVS round S C.	III [VIR A A] A F F; altar.
C. Naevius Capella					
33	AE 13.6 2.595	↑	Qd	C NAEVI[VS CAPELLA]; in centre, S C.	III VI[R A A A F F]; altar.

[26] RICr 427, RIC 186, BMC 209, A 576, BNC 621.
[27] RICr 428, RIC 187, BMC 214, A 586, BNC 621.
[28] RICr 431, RIC 189, BMC 226, A 611, BNC 687.
[29] RICr 431, RIC 189, BMC 226, A 611, BNC 687.
[30] RICr 435, RIC 192, BMC 220, A 592, BNC 654.
[31] RICr 435, RIC 192, BMC 220, A 592, BNC 654.
[32] RICr 466, RIC 215, BMC 265, A 647, BNC 854.
[33] RICr 466, RIC 216, BMC 267, A 650, BNC 863.

No.	Metal Size Weight	Axis	Denomination	Obverse	Reverse
34	AE 15.5 3.045	→	Qd	Similar, but C NAEVIVS CAPELLA.	Similar, but III VIR A A A F F.
C. Rubellius Blandus					
35	AE 14.2 2.260	↙	Qd	C RVBELLIVS BLANDVS; in centre, S C.	III VI[R A] A A F F; altar.
36	AE 14.5 3.300	↙	Qd	Similar, but [C RVBE]-LLIVS BL[ANDVS].	Similar, but [III] VIR [A] A A F F.
A.D. 11–12 Augustus					
37	AE 27.8 11.150	↑	As	IMP CAESAR DIVI F AV-GVSTVS IMP XX; head of Augustus, bare, l.	PONTIF MAXIM TRIBVN POT XXXIIII; in centre, S C.
38	AE 28.4 10.820	↗	As	Similar, but IMP [CAE-SAR] DIVI F AVGVSTVS IMP XX.	Similar, but [PONTIF] MA-XIM TRIBVN POT XXXIIII.
39	AE 27.3 9.350	↓	As	Similar, but [IMP] CAE-SAR DIVI F AVGV[STVS IMP XX].	Similar, but PONTIF MAXIM TRIBVN POT [XXXIIII].

EASTERN MINTS

Mint of Samos (?)
c. 21–20 B.C.

No.	Metal Size Weight	Axis	Denomination	Obverse	Reverse
40	AR 19.7 3.080	↑	D	[CAE]AR; head of Augustus, bare, r.	[AVGVSTVS]; heifer standing r.

---

[34] RICr 466, RIC 216, BMC 267, A 650, BNC 863.
[35] RICr 467, RIC 217, BMC 269, A 652, BNC 868.
[36] RICr 467, RIC 217, BMC 269, A 652, BNC 868.
[37] RICr 471, RIC 219, BMC 275, A 663, BNC 883.
[38] RICr 471, RIC 219, BMC 275, A 663, BNC 883.
[39] RICr 471, RIC 219, BMC 275, A 663, BNC 883.
[40] RICr 475, RIC 59, BMC 662, A 316, BNC 941.

No.	Metal Size Weight	Axis	Denomination	Obverse	Reverse
Mint of Ephesus (?) c. 25 B.C.					
41	AE 26.4 8.720	↗	As	CAESAR; head of Augustus, bare, r.	AUGUSTVS in laurel-wreath.
Mint of Pergamum c. 28–15 B.C.					
42	OR 27.6 13.200	↑	Dp	AVGVSTVS; head of Augustus, bare, r.	C [A] in mixed rostral and laurel-wreath.
Mint of Antioch After 23 B.C.					
43	OR 23.6 13.880	↑	Unit	IMP AV[GVST TR POT]; head of Augustus, laureate, r.	S C in laurel-wreath.

PROVINCIAL ISSUES

HISPANIA CITERIOR

Mint of Celsa
27–12 B.C.
L. Sura
L. Buccus, duumviri

No.	Metal Size Weight	Axis	Denomination	Obverse	Reverse
44	AE 29.0 12.645	↓	As	AVGVSTVS DIVI F; head of Augustus, bare, r.	C V I CEL L SVRA L BV-[CCO] II VIR; bull r.

12–2 B.C.
L. Baccius
Mn. Festus, duumviri

No.	Metal Size Weight	Axis	Denomination	Obverse	Reverse
45	AE 26.7 10.790	↓	As	AVGUSTVS DIVI F; head of Augustus, laureate, r.	[C V I] CEL L BACCIO [MAN] FESTO II VIR; bull r.

[41] RICr 486, RIC 53, BMC 731, A 704, BNC 963.
[42] RICr 502, RIC 50, BMC 721, A 721, BNC 959.
[43] RICr 528, BMC Galatia, Cappadotia, Syria 125, A 750.
[44] A 976, Vives lam. CLX, 12, Villaronga 56.
[45] A 977, Vives lam. CLXI, 1. Villaronga 959.

No.	Metal Size Weight	Axis	Denomination	Obverse	Reverse
Mint of Ilici 13–12 B.C. C. Varus Rufus Sex. Ivl. Pol., duumviri					
46	AE 27.3 10.340	↘	As	AVGVSTVS DIVI F; head of Augustus, laureate, r.	C VAR RVF SEX IVL POL II VIR Q; simpulum, aspergillum, securis, apex.

MACEDONIA

No.	Metal Size Weight	Axis	Denomination	Obverse	Reverse
Mint of Philippi					
47	AE 16.5 4.580	↓	AE	VIC AV[G] across field; Victory on basis, carrying wreath and palm.	COH[OR] PRAE PHIL; three standards.

ACHAEA

No.	Metal Size Weight	Axis	Denomination	Obverse	Reverse
Mint of Corinth 17 B.C. C. Servilius C.f. Primus M. Antonius Hipparchus, duumviri					
48	AE 20.5 6.580	↗	AE	CAE[SAR CORINT] or CORINTHI; head of Augustus, bare, r.	[C SERVILIO C F PRIMO M ANTONIO] HIPPARCHO II VIR; bare heads of Caius and Lucius face to face; between them, C L.
49	AE 19.9 6.700	↙	AE	Similar.	Similar, but [C SERV]ILIO C F PRIMO M [ANTONIO HIPPARCHO II VIR].

JUDEA

No.	Metal Size Weight	Axis	Denomination	Obverse	Reverse
Herold I, 37–4 B.C.					
50	AE 15.1 1.360	↓	AE	[BACI HPWΔ]; anchor.	Double cornucopiae, filleted, with caduceus between.

[46] A 991, Vives lam. CXXXI, 10, Villaronga 992.
[47] A 1100, BMC Macedonia 23.
[48] A 1139, BMC Corinth 505.
[49] A 1139, BMC Corinth 505.
[50] A 869, BMC Palestine 40.

No.	Metal Size Weight	Axis	Deno- mina- tion	Obverse	Reverse
51	AE 15.0 1.800	↓	AE	BACIΛ HPWΔ; anchor.	Similar.

Herod Archelaus, Tetrarcha. 4 B.C.–A.D. 6

No.	Metal Size Weight	Axis	Denomination	Obverse	Reverse
52	AE 16.3 2.550	↓	AE	[HPω]Δϑγ; grapes on branch with wine-leaf.	[EΘNAPXO]; macedonian helmet; to 1. [caduceus].
53	AE 15.3 1.720	↓	AE	Similar.	Similar.

M. Ambibulus, Procurator, c. A.D. 9–12
A.D. 9–10

No.	Metal Size Weight	Axis	Denomination	Obverse	Reverse
54	AE 16.5 2.650	↖	AE	KAICA [POC]; around ear of barley.	Palm tree with two bunches of fruit; in fields, date: [L]M.
55	AE 15.3 1.820	↖	AE	Similar, but KA[ICA] POC.	Similar, but [L M].

SYRIA

Antioch on Orontes
P. Quinctilius Varus, Legatus, 7–8 B.C.
7–6 B.C.

No.	Metal Size Weight	Axis	Denomination	Obverse	Reverse
56	AE 19.3 7.815	↑	AE	Head of Zeus, laureate, r.	ANTIOIOX[ΩN] EΠIOYA-[POY] in r. field, EK; Tyche of Antioch seated r., holding palm.; at her feet, Orontes swimming.

L. Volusius Saturninus, Legatus, A.D. 4–5
A.D. 4–5

No.	Metal Size Weight	Axis	Denomination	Obverse	Reverse
57	AE 19.3 7.915	↑	AE	Head of Zeus, laureate, r.	[AN]TIOX[ΩN] EΠI ΣATO-[PNIN OV]OVOΛO: in r. field, EΛ; Tyche of Antioch seated r., holding palm: at her feet, Orontes swimming.

[51] A 869, BMC Palestine 40.
[52] A 874, BMC Palestine 13.
[53] A 874, BMC Palestine 13.
[54] A 756, BMC Palestine 17.
[55] A 756, BMC Palestine 17.
[56] A 1425, BMC Galatia, Cappadotia, Syria 57.
[57] A 1434, BMC Galatia, Cappadotia, Syria 60.

No.	Metal Size Weight	Axis	Denomination	Obverse	Reverse

Forgeries

Of coin issued by the mint of Caesaraugusta
c. 19–18 B.C.

58	AR 19.2 3.540	↗	D	CAESAR AVGVSTVS; head of Augustus in oak-wreath l.	[DI]VVS – IVLIV[S] to l. and r. of eight-raved comet.

Of coins issued by the mint of Lugdunum
2 B.C. – A.D.14

59	AR 17.7 3.430	↙	D	[CAESAR AVGVSTVS] DIVI F PATER [PATRIAE]; head of Augustus, laureate, r.	C L CAESARES in ex. [AVGVSTI F COS DESIG PRINC IVVENT].
60	AE 19.1 2.220	↑	AE	Similar, but IMP AVGV[STVS DIVI F] PATER PATRIAE.	C L CASAR[ES] in ex. [AVGVSTV F COS DESIG PRINC] IVVENT; Gaius and Lucius Caesares standing front, each togate and resting hand on shield; behind each shield, a spear; above, simpulum and lituus.

A.D. 9–14

61	OR 27.0 10.880	↓	Dp	[CAESAR] AVGVSTVS DIVI F PATER PATRIAE; Head of Augustus, laureate, r.	ROM ET AVG; front elevation of the Altar of Lugdunum, lanked by Victories.

Of coins with Tiberius name

62	AE 34.5 23.130	↓	S	TI CAESAR AVGVST F IMPERATOR V; head of Tiberius, bare, l.	ROM ET AVG; front elevation of the Altar of Lugdunum, lanked by Victories.
63	AE 34.2 29.770	↓	S	Similar.	Similar.
64	AE 22.8 8.030	→	As	[TI CAES]SAR AVGVST F IM [PERAT V] II; head of Tiberius, laureate, r.	Similar.

Of coins issued by the mint of Brundisium and Rome?
c. 32–29 B.C.

65	AR 20.5 3.605	↑	D	Head of Venus r., wearing stephane and necklace.	C CAESAR DIVI F to l. and r. of Octavian in military dress advancing l.; in l. hand, spear, r. extended.

No.	Metal Size Weight	Axis	Deno-mina-tion	Obverse	Reverse
c. 29–27 B.C.					
66	AR 21.4 2.720	↗	D	Head of Octavian, bare, r.	[IMP CAE]SAR to l. and r. of military trophy set on prow with rudder and anchor.
67	AR 19.7 3.770	→	D	Similar.	[IMP] CAESAR; facing quadriga on single arch.
Of coins issued by the mint of Rome 18 B.C.					
T. Quinctius Crispinus Censorinus					
68	AE 23.4 5.600	←	As	AVGVSTV TRIBV P .... (!) in three lines in oak-wreath	....INCFFAA... round Ƨ C.
16 B.C. C. Asinius Gallus					
69	AE 24.4 7.120	↖	As	[CAESAR AVGV]STVS TRIBVNIC POTE[ST]; head of Augustus, bare, r.	C ASINIVS [GALL]VS III VIR [AA] A F F round S C.
C. Gallius Lupercus					
70	AE 25.8 8.550	↘	Dp	AVGVSTV TRIVNIC (!) POTEST in tree lines in oak-wreath.	C GA[LLI]VS III VIR A A A F F round S C.
7 B.C. M. Maecilius Tullus					
71	AE 33.4 25.005	←	Dp ?	CAESAR AVGVST [PONT] MAX TRIBVNIC POT; head of Augustus, laureate, l., crowned by Victory behind bearing cornucopiae; globe at point of bust.	M MAECILIVS TVLLVS III VIR A A A F F round S C.

---

[66] Coin perforated.

No.	Metal Size Weight	Axis	Denomination	Obverse	Reverse

TIBERIUS (A.D. 14–37)

Imperial Issues

GALLIA

Mint of Lugdunum
A.D. 14–37

No.	Metal Size Weight	Axis	Denomination	Obverse	Reverse
72	AR 18.9 3.450	↓	D	TI CAESAR DIVI AVG F AVGVSTVS; head of Tiberius, laureate, r.	PONTIF MAXIM; female figure seated r., holding branch and spear; the chair legs ornamented.

ITALIA

Mint of Rome
A.D. 22–23

No.	Metal Size Weight	Axis	Denomination	Obverse	Reverse
73	AE 32.4 24.645	↙	S	Confronting heads of two little boys on crossed cornucopiae; between, caduceus.	DRVSVS CAESAR TI AVG F DIVI AVG N PONT TR POT II; in centre, S C.
74	AE 29,7 10,870	↓	As	TI CAESAR DIVI AVG F AVGVST IMP VIII; head of Tiberius, bare, 1.	PONTIF MAXIM TRIBVN POTEST XXIIII; in centre, S C.
75	AE 27.6 11.365	↓	As	Similar.	Similar.
76	AE 26.3 11.120	↓	As	Similar.	Similar.
77	AE 29.7 10.410	↑	As	DRVSVS CAESAR TI AVG F DIVI AVG N; head of Drusus, bare, l.	PONTIF TRIBVN PO[TE]ST ITER; in centre, S C.

---

[72] RICr 28, RIC 3, BMC 34.
[73] RICr 42, RIC 28, BMC 95.
[74] RICr 44, RIC 18, BMC 91.
[75] RICr 44, RIC 18, BMC 91.
[76] RICr 44, RIC 18, BMC 91.
[77] RICr 45, RIC 26, BMC 99.

No.	Metal Size Weight	Axis	Denomination	Obverse	Reverse
78	AE 28.1 11.420	↑	As	Similar.	Similar, but PONTIF TRIBVN POTEST ITER.
79	AE 29.2 10.350	↑	As	Similar.	Similar.
80	AE 28.5 9.950	↑	As	Similar, but DRVSVS CAESAR TI AVG F DIVI AVG [N].	Similar, but PONTIF [TRIBVN] POTEST ITER.
81	AE 26.2 9.750	↘	As	Similar, but DRVSV S CAESAR TI AVG F DIVI AVG N.	Similar, but [P]ONTIF TRIBVN POTEST ITER.
82	AE 27.4 13.390	↑	Dp	IVSTITIA; bust of Justitia, diademed, r.	TI CAESAR DIVI AVG F AVG P M TR POT XXIIII in centre, S C.
83	AE 30.5 12.890	↓	Dp	SALVS AVGVSTA; bust of Salus, draped r.; hair in knot behind.	TI CAESAR DIVI AVG F AVG P M TR POT XXIIII in centre, S C.
84	AE 35.7 20.070	→	S	S P Q R IVLIAE AVGVST; carpentum drawn by two mules r., its front and sides ornamented.	TI [CAES]AR DIVI AVG F AVGVST P M TR POT XXIIII; in centre, S C.
A.D. 34–35					
85	AE 27.2 8.850	↑	As	TI C[AESAR] DIVI AVG F AVGVST IMP VIII; head of Tiberius, laureate, l.	PONTIF MAXIM TRIBVN POTEST XXXVI; S – C to l. and r. of vertical winged caduceus.
A.D. 35–36					
86	AE 27.2 10.130	↙	As	TI CAESAR DI[VI] AVG F AVGVST IMP VIII; head of Tiberius, laureate, l.	PONTIF MAX TR POT XXXVII; S – C to l. and r. of rudder placed vertically across banded globe at base of rudder.

78 RICr 45, RIC 26, BMC 99.
79 RICr 45, RIC 26, BMC 99.
80 RICr 45, RIC 26, BMC 99.
81 RICr 45, RIC 26, BMC 99.
82 RICr 46, RIC 22, BMC 79.
83 RICr 47, RIC 23, BMC 81.
84 RICr 51, RIC 21, BMC 76.
85 RICr 53, RIC 40, BMC 106.
86 RICr 58, RIC 39, BMC 117.

No.	Metal Size Weight	Axis	Deno- mina- tion	Obverse	Reverse
87	AE 26.5 10.070	↑	As	TI CAESAR DIVI [AVG F AFGVST] IMP VIII; head of Tiberius, laureate, 1.	PONTIF MAXIM TRIBVN [POTEST XXXVII]; S – C to l. and r. of vertical winged caduceus.
88	AE 26.5 9.965	↗	As	Similar, but[TI CAE]SAR [DIVI] AVG F AVG[VST IMP VIII].	Similar, but PONTIF MAXIM TRIBVN POTEST XXXVII.
89	AE 26.0 10.500	↑	As	Similar, but TI CAESAR DIVI AVG F AV[GVST IMP] VIII.	Similar, but PONTIF MAXIM [TRIBVN] POTEST XXXVII.
DIVVS AVGVSTVS c. A.D. 22/23–30?					
90	AE 27.2 10.240	↙	As	DIVVS AVGVSTVS PATER; head of Augustus, radiate, l.	PROVIDENT in ex; S – C to 1. and r. of square altar.
91	AE 30.0 10.585	↓	As	Similar.	Similar.
92	AE 30.1 9.505	↓	As	Similar.	Similar.
93	AE 30.3 10.390	↓	As	Similar.	Similar.
94	AE 28.7 10.125	↙	As	Similar.	Similar.
95	AE 27.0 10.920	↙	As	Similar, but [DIVVS] AVGVSTVS PATER.	Similar.

[87] RICr 59, RIC 40, BMC 120.
[88] RICr 59, RIC 40, BMC 120.
[89] RICr 59, RIC 40, BMC 120.
[90] RICr 81, RIC 6, BMC 146.
[91] RICr 81, RIC 6, BMC 146.
[92] RICr 81, RIC 6, BMC 146.
[93] RICr 81, RIC 6, BMC 146.
[94] RICr 81, RIC 6, BMC 146.
[95] RICr 81, RIC 6, BMC 146.

No.	Metal Size Weight	Axis	Deno-mina tion	Obverse	Reverse
96	AE 30.0 10.300	↓	As	Similar, but DIVVS AV-GVSTVS PATER.	Similar.
97	AE 27.7 9.665	↘	As	Similar.	Similar.
98	AE 30.8 9.750	↓	As	Similar.	Similar.
99	AE 27.6 9.705	↓	As	Similar.	Similar.
100	AE 27.6 9.705	↓	As	Similar.	Similar.
101	AE 29.0 10.315	↓	As	Similar.	Similar.
102	AE 27.4 9.410	↑	As	Similar, but DIVVS A[V-GVST]VS PATE[R].	Similar.
103	AE 27.4 10.670	↓	As	Similar, but [DIVV]S AV-GVSTVS PATER.	Similar, but [PROVIDEN]T.
104	AE 28.7 11.100	↓	As	Similar, but DIVVS AV-GVSTVS PATER.	Similar, but PROVIDENT.

[96] RICr 81, RIC 6, BMC 146.
[97] RICr 81, RIC 6, BMC 146.
[98] RICr 81, RIC 6, BMC 146.
[99] RICr 81, RIC 6, BMC 146.
[100] RICr 81, RIC 6, BMC 146.
[101] RICr 81, RIC 6, BMC 146.
[102] RICr 81, RIC 6, BMC 146.
[103] RICr 81, RIC 6, BMC 146.
[104] RICr 81, RIC 6, BMC 146.

No.	Metal Size Weight	Axis	Deno-mina-tion	Obverse	Reverse
c. A.D. 34–37					
105	AE 28.4 8.885	↓	As	DIVVS AVGVSTVS PA-TER; head of Augustus, ra-diate, l.	S – C to l. and r. of eagle stg. on globe, head r., wings half-spread.
106	AE 27.0 10.825	↗	As	Similar, but D[IVVS] AV-GVSTVS PATER.	Similar.
107	AE 27.4 10.420	↓	As	Similar, but DIVVS AV-GVSTVS PATER.	Similar.
108	AE 27.2 10.825	↓	As	DIVVS AVGVSTVS PA-TER; head of Augustus, ra-diate, l.	S – C to l. and r. of winged thunderbolt, upright.

Provincial Issues

HISPANIA CITERIOR

Mint of Tarraco

No.	Metal Size Weight	Axis	Deno-mina-tion	Obverse	Reverse
109	AE 21.9 7.550	↙	AE	TI CAESAR DIVI AVG F AVGVSTVS; head of Ti-berius, laureate, r.	DIVVS AVGVSTVS PATER C V T TAR; head of Augustus, radiate, r.

JUDEA

Pontius Pilatus, Procurator, A.D. 26–36
A.D. 29–30

No.	Metal Size Weight	Axis	Deno-mina-tion	Obverse	Reverse
110	AE 15.9 2.330	→	AE	[IO]YΛIA KAICAPOC; three cars of barley, central upright, tied together.	TIBЄRIO K[AICAPOCLI]; vessel resembling a simpulum with upright handle on r.
111	AE 15.5 2.200	↘	AE	Similar, but [IO]YΛ-IA [KAICAPOC].	Similar, but TI[BЄPIOY] KAIC[APCLIς].

[105] RICr 82, RIC 3, BMC 155.
[106] RICr 82, RIC 3, BMC 155.
[107] RICr 82, RIC 3, BMC 155.
[108] RICr 83, RIC 1, BMC 157.
[109] C. 213, Vives, lam. CLXXI, 5, Villaronga 1052.
[110] BMC Palestine 54.
[111] BMC Palestine 54.

No.	Metal Size Weight	Axis	Denomination	Obverse	Reverse
A.D. 30–31					
112	AE 15.0 2.000	↗	AE	TIB[ЄPIO KAICAPOC]; lituus r.	Wreath with berries; in centre, date: LIZ
A.D. 31–32					
113	AE 14.7 2.320	↑		[TIBЄPIO KAICAPOC]; lituus r.	Wreath with berries; in centre, date: LIH

Forgeries

Of coins issued by the mint of Lugdunum
c. A.D. 14–37

No.	Metal Size Weight	Axis	Denomination	Obverse	Reverse
114	AR 19.0 3.060	↓	D	[TI CAESAR DIVI AVG] F AVGVS[TVS]; head of Tiberius, laureate, r.	PONTIF MAXIM; female figure seated r., holding branch and spear; the chair legs ornamented.
115	AE 36.3 23.630	↓	S	TI CAESAR DIVI AVG F; head of Tiberius, bare, l.	ROM ET AVG; altar of Lugdunum flanked by Victories.

Of coins issued by the mint of Rome
A.D. 15–34

No.	Metal Size Weight	Axis	Denomination	Obverse	Reverse
116	AE 29.3 13.670	↑	Dp	SALVS AVGVSTA; bust of Salus, draped, r.; hair in knot behind.	TI CAESAR DIVI AVG F AVG P M TR POT XXIIII; in centre, S C.
117	AE 30.5 7.670	↑	As	TI CAESAR DIV[I AVG F] AVGVST IMP VII; head of Tiberius, bare, l.	[PON]TIF MAXIM [TRIBVN POTEST XVII]; S – C to l. and r.: female figure, draped, seated r., holding patera and sceptre.

DIVVS AVGVSTVS

No.	Metal Size Weight	Axis	Denomination	Obverse	Reverse
118	AE 33.7 18.650	↓	S	DIVVS AVGVSTVS PATER; head of Augustus, laureate, l.	S – C to l. and r.; shield inscribed OB CIVES SER surround by oak-wreath supported by capricorns; globe below.

[112] BMC Palestine 69.
[113] BMC Palestine 81.
[117] Coin perforated.
[118] Coin perforated.

No.	Metal Size Weight	Axis	Denomination	Obverse	Reverse
119	AE 28.2 8.310	↓	As	[DIVVS] AV GVSTVS PATE[R]; head of Augustus radiate, l.	[P]ROVIDENT; S – C to l. and r. of square altar.
120	AE 27.0 7.100	↓	As	Similar, but DIV[VS AV]GV [STVS] PATER.	Similar.
121	AE 25.5 9.600	↑	As	Similar, but [DIV]VS AVGVSTVS PATER.	S – C to l. and r. of winged thunderbolt.

Of coin issued by the mint of Ilici
M. Iulius Setal
L. Sest. Celer, duumviri

No.	Metal Size Weight	Axis	Denomination	Obverse	Reverse
122	AE 27.3 10.775	↖	AE	TI CAESAR DIVI AVG F AVGVSTVS P M; head of Tiberius, bare, l.	M IVLIVS SETAL L SEST CELER IIVIR; rectangular altar inscribed: SAL AVG.

GAIUS (A.D. 37–41)

Imperial Issues

Mint of Rome
A.D. 37–38

No.	Metal Size Weight	Axis	Denomination	Obverse	Reverse
123	AE 28.5 12.100	↓	Dp	[N]ERO ET DRVSVS CAESA[RES]; Nero and Drusus Caesar riding r., cloaks flying.	C [CAESAR A]VG GERMANICVS PON M TR POT round S C.
124	AE 28.7 13.200	↓	Dp	Similar, but [NERO] ET DRVSVS C[AESARES].	Similar, but C CAESAR [AVG] GERMANICVS PON M TR POT.
125	AE 27.4 11.000	↙	As	[GER]MANICVS CAESAR TI AVGVST F DIVI AVG N; head of Germanicus, bare, l.	C CAESAR AVG GERMANICVS PON M TR POT round S C.
126	AE 28.4 10.825	↙	As	Similar, but GERMANICVS CAESAR TI AVGVST DIVI AVG N.	Similar, but C CAESAR AVG GERMANICVS PON [M TR POT].

[123] RICr 34, RIC 43, BMC 44.
[124] RICr 34, RIC 43, BMC 44.
[125] RICr 35, RIC 44, BMC 49.
[126] RICr 35, RIC 44, BMC 49.

No.	Metal Size Weight	Axis	Deno-mina-tion	Obverse	Reverse
127	AE 26.8 10.150	↙	As	[C C]AESAR AVG GERMANICVS PON M TR [POT]; head of Gaius, bare, l.	[VESTA] above; S – C to l. and r. of Vesta, veiled, seated l. on throne, holding patera and long sceptre.
128	AE 28.6 10.710	↓	As	Similar, but C CAESAR AVG GERMANICVS PON M TR POT.	Similar, but VESTA.
129	AE 29.7 11.170	↙	As	Similar.	Similar, but V[ES]TA.
A.D. 40–41					
130	AE 28.8 10.600	↓	As	GERMANICVS CAESAR TI AVG F DIVI AVG N; head of Germanicus, bare, l.	C CAESAR DIVI AVG PRON AVG P M TR P IIII P P round S C.
131	AE 27.7 11.370	↓	As	C CAESAR DIVI AVG PRON AVG P M TR P IIII P P; head of Gaius, bare, l.	VESTA above; S – C to l. and r. of Vesta, veiled, seated 1. on throne, holding patera and long sceptre.
132	AE 28.6 9.770	↓	As	Similar.	Similar.
133	AE 16.7 3.230	↓	Quad.	C CAESAR DIVI AVG PRON AVG; S – C to l. and r. of pileus.	PON M TR P IIII P P COS TERT round R C C.
A.D. 41					
134	AE 17.5 3.640	↓	Quad.	C CAESAR DIVI AVG PRON AVG; S – C to l. and r. of pileus.	PON M TR P IIII P P COS QVAT round R C C.

[127] RICr 38, RIC 30, BMC 45.
[128] RICr 38, RIC 30, BMC 45.
[129] RICr 38, RIC 30, BMC 45.
[130] RICr 50, RIC 47, BMC 74.
[131] RICr 54, RIC 32, BMC 72.
[132] RICr 54, RIC 32, BMC 72.
[133] RICr 52, RIC 40, BMC 64.
[134] RICr –, RIC 41, BMC 79.

No.	Metal Size Weight	Axis	Denomination	Obverse	Reverse
Undated					
135	AE 28.2 15.580	↓	Dp	GERMANIC[VS] CAESAR: Germanicus, bare-headed and cloaked, standing in slow quadriga r., holding eagle-tipped sceptre.	SIGNIS RECE[PT] DEVICTIS GER[M]; S – C; Germanicus, bare-headed and cuirassed with tunic, standing l., raided r. hand, in l. holding aquila.
136	AE 28.3 13.320	↓	As	M AGRIPPA L F COS III; head of Agrippa l., wearing rostral crown.	S – C to l. and r. of Neptune standing l., cloaked, holding small dolphin in r. hand, in l., vertical trident.
137	AE 28.4 10.220	↙	As	Similar.	Similar.
138	AE 30.5 10.000	↓	As	Similar.	Similar.
139	AE 28.0 10.670	↓	As	Similar.	Similar.
140	AE 26.2 10.150	↓	As	Similar, but M AGRIPPA L [F] COS III.	Similar.
141	AE 28.4 11.920	↓	As	Similar, but M AGRIPPA L F COS III.	Similar.
142	AE 29.5 10.395	↙	As	Similar.	Similar.

[135] RICr 57, RIC s. 119, BMC 94.
[136] RICr 58, RIC 32, BMC (Tiberius) 161.
[137] RICr 58, RIC 32, BMC (Tiberius) 161.
[138] RICr 58, RIC 32, BMC (Tiberius) 161.
[139] RICr 58, RIC 32, BMC (Tiberius) 161.
[140] RICr 58, RIC 32, BMC (Tiberius) 161.
[141] RICr 58, RIC 32, BMC (Tiberius) 161; coin perforated.
[142] RICr 58, RIC 32, BMC (Tiberius) 161.

No.	Metal Size Weight	Axis	Denomination	Obverse	Reverse
143	AE 27.9 10.585	↙	As	Similar.	Similar.
144	AE 26.0 8.315	→	As	Similar, but [M] AGRIPPA L F COS III.	Similar.
145	AE 26.9 10.585	↓	As	Similar, but M AGRIPPA L F COS III.	Similar.

DIVVS AVGVSTVS

No.	Metal Size Weight	Axis	Denomination	Obverse	Reverse
146	AE 27.9 12.130	↓	Dp	DIVVS AVGVSTVS; S – C to l. and r. of head of Augustus, radiate, l.	CONSENSV SENAT ET EQ ORDIN P Q R; Augustus? laureate and togate, seated l., on curule chair, holding branch in r. hand, l. against side.

Provincial Issues

HISPANIA TARRACONENSIS

Mint of Caesaraugusta
A.D. 37
Germano
Liciniano, duumviri

No.	Metal Size Weight	Axis	Denomination	Obverse	Reverse
147	AE 30.9 12.240	↓	As	C·CAESAR·AVG·GERMANICVS·IMP; head of Gaius, laureate, l.	LICINIANO·ET·GERMANO·II·VIR; priest ploughing r.; above, C·C·A.
148	AE 28.9 12.175	↘	As	Similar.	Similar.

[143] RICr 58, RIC 32, BMC (Tiberius) 161.
[144] RICr 58, RIC 32, BMC (Tiberius) 161.
[145] RICr 58, RIC 32, BMC (Tiberius) 161.
[146] RICr 56, RIC 8, BMC 88.
[147] C. 43, Vives, lam. CLIV, 6; Villaronga 294.
[148] C. 43, Vives, lam. CLIV, 6; Villaronga 294.

No.	Metal Size Weight	Axis	Deno-mina-tion	Obverse	Reverse

Forgeries

Of coins issued by the mint of Rome
A.D. 37–41

No.	Metal Size Weight	Axis	Denomination	Obverse	Reverse
149	AE 33.6 26.150	↓	S	C CAESAR AVG GERMANICVS PON M TR POT; head of Gaius, laureate, l.	S P Q R P P OB CIVES SERVATOS in four lines in oak-wreath.
150	AE 33.0 25.150	↓	S	C CAESAR AVG GERMANICVS PON M TR POT; head of Gaius, laureate, l.	A[GRIPPINA] DRVSILLA IVLIA; S C in ex. Gaius three sisters standing facing, personified as Securitas, Concordia and Fortuna.
151	AE 26.2 8.380	↙	As	C CAESAR AVG GERMANICVS [PON M] TR POT; head of Gaius, bare, l.	[VESTA] above; S – C to l. and r. of Vesta, veiled, seated l. on throne, holding patera and long sceptre.
152	AE 27.6 9.700	↓	As	Similar, but C CAESAR DIVI AVG PRON AVG P M TR P III P P.	Similar, but VESTA.
153	AE 28,3 10.520	↓	As	GERMANICVS CAESAR TI AVG F DIVI A[VG] N; head of Germanicus, bare, l.	C CAESAR DIVI AVG PRON AVG P M TR P III P P round S C.
154	AE 28.1 8.430	↓	As	Similar, but GERMANICVS CAESAR TI AVG F DIVI [AVG N].	Similar.
155	AE 25.8 10.230	↖	As	Similar, but GERMAN CVS CAESAR TI AVGVST DIVI AVG N (!).	Similar, but C CAESAR AVG GERMANICVS PON M TR POT.
156	AE 20.5 5.420	↓	AE	C CAESAR AVG GERM P M TR POT; head of Gaius, laureate, r.	GERMANICVS CAES P C CAES AVG GERM; head of Germanicus, bare, r.
157	AE 30.0 10.990	↓	As	M AGRIPPA L F COS III; head of Agrippa, wearing rostral crown, l.	S – C to l. and r. of Neptune standing l., cloaked, holding in r. hand small dolphin, in l., vertical trident.

[157] Coin perforated.

No.	Metal Size Weight	Axis	Denomination	Obverse	Reverse
158	AE 28.3 9.420	↓	As	Similar.	Similar.

CLAUDIUS (A.D. 41–54)

Imperial Issues

Mint of Rome
25 January 41 – 3 December 41

No.	Metal Size Weight	Axis	Denomination	Obverse	Reverse
159	AE 16.7 3.370	↑	Quad	TI CLAVDIVS CAESAR AVG; modius.	PON M TR P IMP COS DES IT; in centre, S C.
160	AE 17.8 2.710	↗	Quad	Similar.	Similar.
161	AE 17.6 3.140	↑	Quad	Similar, but TI CLA [VD-IV]S [CA]ESAR AVG.	Similar.
162	AE 17.3 3.730	↙	Quad	TI CL[AVDIVS C]AESAR AVG; hand l., holding pair of scales; above, P N R.	PON M TR P IMP COS DES IT; in centre, S C.
163	AE 14.7 4.000	↙	Quad	Similar, but TI CLAV-DIVS [CAESAR AVG].	Similar, but [PON M TR P IMP] COS DES IT.

5 January 42 – 31 December 42

No.	Metal Size Weight	Axis	Denomination	Obverse	Reverse
164	AE 17.3 2.770	↑	Quad	TI CLAVDIVS CAESAR AVG; modius.	PON M TR P IMP P P COS II; in centre, S C.

---

159 RICr 84, RIC 72, BMC 173.
160 RICr 84, RIC 72, BMC 173.
161 RICr 84, RIC 72, BMC 173.
162 RICr 85, RIC 74, BMC 174.
163 RICr 85, RIC 74, BMC 174.
164 RICr 90, RIC 72, BMC 182.

No.	Metal Size Weight	Axis	Deno-mina-tion	Obverse	Reverse
165	AE 17.3 3.370	↑	Quad	Similar, but [TI CL]AV-DIVS CAESAR AV[G].	Similar.
166	AE 17.1 3.070	↗	Quad	Similar, but TI CLAVDIVS CAESAR AVG.	Similar.
Undated coins c. A.D. 41–50					
167	AE 36.2 27.140	↓	S	NERO CLAVDIVS [DRV]-SVS GERMANICVS IMP; head of Nero Claudius Drusus, bare, l.	TI CLAVDIVS CAESAR AVG P M TR P IMP; in ex. S C; Claudius, seated l. on curule chair, holding out branch in r. hand; miscellaneous weapons and armour lying around.
168	AE 30.9 11.195	↓	As	TI CLAVDIVS CAESAR AVG P M TR P IMP; head of Claudius, bare, l.	CONSTANTIAE AVGVSTI; S – C to l. and r. of Constantia, helmeted and in military dressed standing l., raised r. hand, in l. holding long spear.
169	AE 30.0 8.980	↓	As	TI CLAVDIVS CAESAR AVG P M TR [P IMP]; head of Claudius, bare, l.	LIBERTAS AVGVSTA; S – C to l. and r. Libertas., dr., standing facing, head r., holding pileus in r. hand, l. extended
170	AE 28.3 11.190	↙	As	Similar, but TI CLAVDIVS CAESAR AVG P M TR P IMP.	Similar.
DIVUS AUGUSTUS					
171	AE 29.8 13.020	↓	Dp	DIVVS AVGVSTVS; S – C to l. and r. head of Augustus, radiate, l.	DIVA AVGVSTA; Livia seated l., holding corn-ears in r. hand, l. long torch.

[165] RICr 90, RIC 72, BMC 182.
[166] RICr 90, RIC 72, BMC 182.
[167] RICr 93, RIC 78, BMC 157.
[168] RICr 95, RIC 68, BMC 140.
[169] RiCr 97, RIC 69, BMC 145.
[170] RICr 97, RIC 69, BMC 145.
[171] RICr 101, RIC 9, BMC 224.

No.	Metal Size Weight	Axis	Deno-mina-tion	Obverse	Reverse
c. A.D. 50–54					
172	AE 36.8 29.750	↓	S	AGRIPPINA M F GERMANICI CAESARIS; bust of Agrippina (senior), dr., r.; head bare, hair in long plait.	TI CLAVDIVS CAESAR AVG GERM P M TR P IMP P P; in centre, S C.
173	AE 30.5 16.150	↓	Dp	ANTONIA AVGVSTA; bust of Antonia, dr., r.; head bare, hair in long plait.	TI CLAVDIVS CAESAR AVG P M TR P IMP P P; Claudius, veiled and togate, standing l., holding simpulum; S – C to 1. and r.
174	AE 29.2 11.170	↓	As	TI CLAVDIVS CAESAR P M TR P IMP P [P]; head of Claudius, bare, l.	CONSTA[NTIAE] AVGVSTI; S – C to 1. and r. of Constantia, helmeted and in military dress, standing 1., raised r. hand, in 1. holding long spear.
175	AE 30.0 12.440	↓	As	TI CLAVDIVS CAESAR AVG P M TR P IMP P P; head of Claudius, bare, l.	LIBERTAS AVGVSTA; S – C to 1. and r. of Libertas, draped, standing facing head r., holding pileus in r. hand, 1. extended.
176	AE 29.2 11.970	↓	As	Similar.	Similar.
177	AE 29.8 11.380	↓	As	Similar.	Similar.
178	AE 29.4 10.350	↘	As	TI CLAVDIVS CAESAR AVG P M TR P IMP PP; head of Claudius, bare, 1.	S – C to l. and r. of Minerva r., helmeted and draped; r. hand hurling javelin, round shield on l. arm.
179	AE 29.6 9.900	↙	As	Similar.	Similar.

[172] RICr 102, RIC 85, BMC 219.
[173] RICr 104, RIC 82, BMC 213.
[174] RICr 111, RIC 68, BMC 199.
[175] RICr 113, RIC 69, BMC 204.
[176] RICr 113, RIC 69, BMC 204.
[177] RICr 113, RIC 69, BMC 204.
[178] RICr 116, RIC 66, BMC 206.
[179] RICr 116, RIC 66, BMC 206.

No.	Metal Size Weight	Axis	Deno-mina-tion	Obverse	Reverse
180	AE 29.7 10.150	↙	As	Similar.	Similar.
181	AE 28.8 11.250	↓	As	Similar.	Similar.

Provincial Imitations of Imperial Bronze Coins

GALLIA

No.	Metal Size Weight	Axis	Deno-mina-tion	Obverse	Reverse
182	AE 25.9 11.525	↓	As	[TI CL]AVDIVS CAESAR AVG P M TR [P IMP]; head of Claudius, bare l.	[CONSTANTIAE] AVGVSTI; S – C to l. and r. of Constantia, helmeted and in military dress, standing l., raised r. han[d], in l. holding long spear.
183	AE 29.7 10.160	↓	As	Similar, but TI CLAVDIVS CAESAR AVG P M TR P IMP P P.	Similar.
184	AE 29.3 8.870	↓	As	Similar, but TI CLAV-DIVS CAESAR AVG P M TR P IMP.	LIB[ERTAS] AVGVSTA; S – C to l. and r. of Libertas, draped, standing facing, head r., holding pileus in r. hand, l. extended.
185	AE 29.6 10.900	↙	As	Similar.	Similar, but LIBERTAS AV-GVSTA.
186	AE 27.3 9.890	↓	As	Similar.	Similar.
187	AE 28.9 10.500	↓	As	Similar, but TI CLAV-DIVS CAESAR AVG P M TR [P IMP].	Similar.

---

[180] RICr 116, RIC 66, BMC 206.
[181] RICr 116, RIC 66, BMC 206.
[183] BMC 143, 144.
[184] BMC 147.
[185] BMC 147, 148.

No.	Metal Size Weight	Axis	Denomination	Obverse	Reverse

HISPANIA

No.	Metal Size Weight	Axis	Denomination	Obverse	Reverse
188	AE 29.4 9.660	↓	As	TI CLAVDIVS CAESAR AVG P M TR P IMP; head of Claudius, bare, l.	S – C to l. and r. of Minerva r., helmeted and draped; r. hand hurling javelin; round shield on l. arm.
189	AE 26.4 6.810	↙	As	Similar, but TI CLAVDIVS CAESAR AVG P M TR P IMP.	Similar, [S C].
190	AE 28.2 8.760	↙	As	Similar, but TI CLAVDIVS CAESAR AVG P M TR P IMP P P.	Similar, but S – C.
191	AE 29.0 10.900	↙	As	Similar.	Similar.
192	AE 24.7 6.655	↘	As	[M AGRIPPA L F] COS III; head of Agrippa l., wearing rostral crown.	S – C to l. and r. of Neptune standing l., cloaked, holding small dolphin in r. hand, in l., vertical trident.

Provincial Issues

JUDEA

Herod Agrippa I, A.D. 37–44
A.D. 42–43

No.	Metal Size Weight	Axis	Denomination	Obverse	Reverse
193	AE 17.7 2.560	↑	AE	BACI[ΛЄωC ΑΓΡΙΠΑ]; umbrella with fringe.	Date: L[ξ] across field: three ears of barley issuing from between two leaves.
194	AE 17.1 3.100	↑	AE	Similar, but [BACIΛЄ]ωC ΑΓΡ[ΙΠΑ].	Similar, but [Lς].
195	AE 17.1 2.890	↖	AE	Similar, but [BACIΛЄ]ωC ΑΓΡ[ΙΠΑ].	Similar, but L[ς].

---

[188] BMC 150.
[193] BMC Palestine 1–18.
[194] BMC Palestine 1–18.
[195] BMC Palestine 1–18.

No.	Metal Size Weight	Axis	Denomination	Obverse	Reverse
196	AE 17.1 2.715	↑	AE	Similar, but [BA]CIΛЄωC ΑΓΡΙ[ΠΑ].	Similar.
197	AE 16.8 2.510	↑	AE	Similar, but [BACIΛЄ]ωC ΑΓΡΙΠΑ.	Similar, but L ξ.
198	AE 17.5 2.370	↑	AE	Similar, but BACIΛ[ЄωC ΑΓΡΙΠΑ].	Similar, but L[ς].
199	AE 16.2 2.020	↑	AE	Similar, but BACIΛЄω[C ΑΓΡΙΠΑ].	Similar, but [Lς].
200	AE 17.6 2.475	↑	AE	Similar, but BACIΛЄ[ω-C ΑΓΡΙΠΑ].	Similar, but L[ς].
201	AE 16.1 2.270	↗	AE	Similar, but BACIΛЄωC [ΑΓΡΙΠΑ].	Similar.
202	AE 17.1 2.745	↑	AE	Similar, but BACI[ΛЄωC ΑΓΡΙΠΑ].	Similar
203	AE 17.1 2.470	↑	AE	Similar, but BACIΛЄω[C ΑΓΡΙΠΑ].	Similar, but Lς
204	AE 18.1 2.640	↑	AE	Similar, but BACIΛЄω[C ΑΓΡΙΠΑ].	Similar, but L[ς].
205	AE 16.8 2.250	↑	AE	Similar, but [BACIΛЄωC ΑΓ]ΡΙΠΑ.	Similar, but [L] ς.

[196] BMC Palestine 1–18.
[197] BMC Palestine 1–18.
[198] BMC Palestine 1–18.
[199] BMC Palestine 1–18.
[200] BMC Palestine 1–18.
[201] BMC Palestine 1–18.
[202] BMC Palestine 1–18.
[203] BMC Palestine 1–18.
[204] BMC Palestine 1–18.
[205] BMC Palestine 1–18.

No.	Metal Size Weight	Axis	Deno-mina-tion	Obverse	Reverse
206	AE 16.8 2.500	↑	AE	Similar, but [ΒΑϹΙΛ]ЄΩϹ ΑΓΡΙΠΑ.	Similar.

Forgeries

Of coins issued by the mint of Rome

No.	Metal Size Weight	Axis	Deno-mina-tion	Obverse	Reverse
207	AE 26.6 10.920	↙	Dp	A NTONIA AVGV STA; bust of Antonia, draped, r.; head bare, hair in long plait.	[TI CLAVDIVS] CAESAR [AVG P M TR P IMP P P]; S – C to l. and r. of Claudius, veiled and togate, standing l., holding simpulum.
208	AE 29.8 17.400	↓	Dp	Similar, but ANTONIA AV-GVSTA.	Similar, but TI CLAVDIVS CAESAR AVG P M TR P IMP P P.
209	AE 27.1 7.850	↘	As	TI CLAVDIVS CAESAR AVG P M TR P IMP P P; head of Claudius, bare, l.	[LIBE]RTAS AVGVS[TA]; S – C to l. and r. of Libertas, draped, standing facing, head r., holding pileus in r. hand, l. extended.
210	AE 29.3 9.700	↓	As	Similar.	Similar, but LIBERTAS AV-GVSTA.
211	AE 28.5 8.970	↓	As	Similar.	S – C to l. and r. of Minerva r., helmeted and draped; r. hand hurling javelin; round shield on l. arm.

NERO (A.D. 54–68)

Imperial Issues

Mint of Rome

Undated, post-reform denarii

c. A.D. 64–65

No.	Metal Size Weight	Axis	Deno-mina-tion	Obverse	Reverse
212	AR 18.1 3.020	↘	D	[NE]RO CAESAR AVGV-STVS; head of Nero, laure-ate, r.	[IVPPITER CVSTOS]; Jupiter, bare to waist, seated l. on throne, holding thunderbolt in r. hand, in l. long sceptre.

[206] BMC Palestine 1–18.

[212] RICr 53, RIC 45, BMC 74.

No.	Metal Size Weight	Axis	Deno-mina-tion	Obverse	Reverse
213	AR 18.9 3.050	↓	D	NERO CAESAR AVG[V-STVS]; head of Nero, laureate, r.	ROMA (ex.); Roma, seated l. on cuirass, holding Victory in r. hand, in l. parazonium by side; r. foot resting on helmet.
c. A.D. 65–66					
214	AR 18.1 2.790	↓	D	NERO CAESAR AVGV-STVS; head of Nero, laureate, r.	[V]EST[A] above round, domed, hexastyle temple with four steps; within, Vesta, seated, holding patera and long sceptre.
c. A.D. 67 – 68					
215	AR 18.0 3.300	↘	D	[IMP] NERO CAESAR AVG P P; head of Nero, laureate, r.	[IV]PPITER CVSTOS; Jupiter, bare to waist, seated l. on throne, holding thunderbolt in r. hand, in l. long sceptre.

AES

Issue III
c. A.D. 64

No.	Metal Size Weight	Axis	Deno-mina-tion	Obverse	Reverse
216	Orch 29.7 15.740	↓	Dp	NERO CLAVD CAESAR AVG GER P M TR P [P P]; head of Nero, radiate, r.	VICTORIA AVGVSTI; S – C to r. and l. of Victory flying l., r. leg advanced, holding wreath in r. hand, in l. palm; in ex. II.
Issue IV c. A.D. 65					
217	AE 35.1 25.830	↓	S	NERO CLAVD CAESAR AVG GER P M TR P IMP P P; head of Nero, laureate, r.	ROMA; S – C to l. and r. of Roma, helmeted and in military dress, seated l. on cuirass, holding Victory in r. hand, l. resting on parazonium.
218	AE 27.4 9.270	↓	As	NERO CAESAR AVG GERM IMP; head of Nero, laureate, r.	PACE P R VBIQ PARTA IANVM CLVSIT; front of the temple of Janus, with latticed window to l. and closed double doors to r. S – C to l. and r.

[213] RICr 55, RIC 50, BMC 83.
[214] RICr 62, RIC 58, BMC 104.
[215] RICr 69, RIC 47, BMC 80.
[216] RICr 196, RIC 308, BMC 214.
[217] RICr 276, RIC 206, BMC 173.
[218] RICr 306, RIC 198, BMC 227.

No.	Metal Size Weight	Axis	Denomination	Obverse	Reverse
219	AE 27.4 11.650	↓	As	Similar.	Similar.
220	AE 27.1 9.540	↓	As	Similar.	Similar.
221	AE 29.2 10.100	↓	As	Similar, but head of Nero l.	Similar.
222	AE 26.2 9.550	↓	As	NERO CAESAR AVG GERM IMP; head of Nero, laureate, r.	S – C to l. and r. of Victory flying l., holding in both hands shield inscribed S[PQR].
223	AE 30.0 11.280	↓	As	Similar.	Similar.
224	AE 28.5 11.495	↓	As	Similar.	Similar, but [SPQR].
225	AE 26.3 12.195	↓	As	Similar.	Similar.
226	AE 29.1 9.550	↓	As	Similar.	Similar.
227	AE 28.4 10.650	↓	As	Similar, but [NE]RO CAESAR AVG GERM IMP.	Similar.
228	AE 26.3 8.050	↓	As	Similar, but [NERO CAES]AR AVG GERM IMP.	Similar.

[219] RICr 306, RIC 198, BMC 227.
[220] RICr 306, RIC 198, BMC 227.
[221] RICr 307, RIC 198, BMC 228.
[222] RICr 312, RIC 318, BMC 241.
[223] RICr 312, RIC 318, BMC 241.
[224] RICr 312, RIC 318, BMC 241.
[225] RICr 312, RIC 318, BMC 241.
[226] RICr 312, RIC 318, BMC 241.
[227] RICr 313, RIC 318, BMC 245; coin perforated.
[228] RICr 315, RIC 318, BMC 245.

No.	Metal Size Weight	Axis	Deno-mina-tion	Obverse	Reverse
Issue V c. A.D. 66					
229	AE 25.0 21.540	↓	As	IMP NERO CLAVD CAESAR AVG GER P M TR P P P; head of Nero, laureate, r.	PACE P R [TERRA MARIQ] PARTA IANVM CLVSIT; S – C to l. and r., front of the temple of Janus, with latticed window to l. and closed double doors to r.
230	AE 26.6 8.950	↓	As	IMP NERO CAESAR AVG GERM; head of Nero, laureate, l.	[PACE] P R VBIQ PARTA IANVM CLVSIT; S – C to l. and r., front of the temple of Janus, with latticed window to l. and closed double doors to r.
231	AE 25.7 10.000	↓	As	Similar, but head of Nero, r.	Similar, but PACE P R VBIQ PARTA IANVMCLV-SIT.
Mint of Lugdunum Issue II c. A.D. 65					
232	AE 34.2 23.240	↓	S	NERO CLAVD CAE-SAR AVG GER P M TR P I[MP P P]; head of Nero, laureate, r.	ANNONA AVGVSTI [CE]-RES; S C in ex.; Ceres, veiled and drapel, seated l., holding corn-ears and torch, her feet on stool; facing Annona, stand-ing r., resting r. hand on hip, l. holding corcnucopiae; between them, modius on altar; behind, ship's stern.
233	AE 30.4 13.295	↓	Dp	[NERO] CLAVD CAE-SAR AVG GER P M TR P IM[P P P]; head of Nero, laureate, l.	VICTOR[IA] AVGVSTI; II in ex.; S – C to l. and r. of Victoria walking l., holding wreath in r. hand, in l. palm.

[229] RICr 324, RIC 182, BMC 163.
[230] RICr 348, RIC 203, BMC 231.
[231] RICr 349, RIC 194, BMC 226
[232] RICr 390, RIC 77, BMC 305.
[233] RICr 412, RIC 306, BMC 350.

No.	Metal Size Weight	Axis	Denomination	Obverse	Reverse
Issue III c. A.D. 65					
234	AE 36.0 22.070	↓	S	NERO CLAVD CAESAR AVG GER P M TR P IMP P P; head of Nero, laureate, l.; globe at point of bust.	D[E]C[VRSIO]; S – C to l. and r. of Nero, prancing r. on horseback, holding spear in r. hand; behind him, mounted soldier prancing r. with vexillium over l. shoulder.
Issue IV c. A.D. 66					
235	Orch 29.2 12.280	↓	Dp	IMP NERO CAESAR AVG P MAX TR P P P; head of Nero, laureate, l.; globe at point of bust.	VICTORIA AVGVSTI; S – C to l. and r. of Victory walking l., holding wreath in r. hand, in l. palm.
236	AE 28.7 9.690	↓	As	IMP NERO CAESAR AVG P [MAX TR] P P P; head of Nero, bare, r.; globe at point of bust.	S – C to l. and r. of Victory flying l., holding in r. hand shield inscribed S[PQR].
237	AE 29.0 9.390	↓	As	Similar, but IMP CAESAR AVG P MAX [TR P P P].	Similar.
238	AE 27.6 9.950	↓	As	Similar, but IMP NERO CAESAR AVG P M[AX T]R P [P P], head of Nero l.	Similar.
Issue V c. A.D. 67					
239	AE 25.5 21.320	↓	S	[IMP] NERO CAESAR AVG P MAX [TR POT P P]; head of Nero, laureate, l.; globe at point of bust.	S – C to l. and r. of triumphal arch, surmounted by facing quadriga escorted on r. by Victory and on l. by Pax; on l. side of arch in niche, figure of Mars standing facing, holding spear and shield.

---

[234] RICr 437, RIC 139, BMC –
[235] RICr 523, RIC 304, BMC 356.
[236] RICr 540, RIC 329, BMC 381.
[237] RICr 540, RIC 329, BMC 381.
[238] RICr 542, RIC 329, BMC 387.
[239] RICr 575, RIC 156, BMC 331.

No.	Metal Size Weight	Axis	Denomination	Obverse	Reverse
Mint of Antioch					
240	Orch 20.0 6.720	↑	Unit	IM NER CLAV [CAESAR]; head of Nero, laureate, r.	S C in laurel-wreath.

Provincial Issues

Aegyptus

Mint of Alexandria
A.D. 63/64, year 10

No.	Metal Size Weight	Axis	Denomination	Obverse	Reverse
241	AR 24.4 12.500	↑	Tetrdr.	[ΝΕΡΩΚΛΑΥ] ΚΑΙΣΣΕΒΓΕΡ; head of Nero, radiate, r.	ΑΥ[ΤΟ] ΚΡΑ; in front, LI; bust of Sarapis r., wearing taenia and modius adorned with laurel-branches.
242	AR 26.5 11.930	↑	Tetrdr.	Similar, but ΝΕ[ΡΩΚΛΑ] ΥΚΑΙΣΣΕΒΓΕΡ.	Similar, but ΑΥΤΟ Κ[ΡΑ].
A.D. 64/65, year 11					
243	AR 23.1 12.000	↗	Tetrdr.	ΝΕΡΩΚ[ΛΑΥΚ] ΑΙΣΣΕΒΓΕΡ; bust of Neron r., radiate, wearing aegis.	ΑΥΤΟΚΡΑ, in front, LIA; eagle l., on thunderbolt; behind eagle, palm.
244	AR 24.4 10.200	↗	Tetrdr.	Similar, but [Ν]Ε[Ρ]ΩΚΛΑΥ [ΚΑΙ]ΣΣΕΒΓΕΡ.	Similar, but [ΑΥΤΟ] ΚΡΑ.
245	AR 25.0 11.920	↑	Tetrdr.	Similar, but ΝΕΡΟΚΛΑΥΚ [ΑΙ]ΣΣΕΒΓΕΡ.	Similar, but Α[ΥΤ]ΟΚΡΑ.
246	AR 22.2 9.870	↑	Tetrdr.	[ΝΕΡΩΚΛΑΥΚΑΙΣΣΕΒΓΕΡ]; head of Nero, radiate, r.	[ΑΥΤΟ] ΚΡΑ, in front LIA; bust of Sarapis r., wearing taenia and modius adorned with laurel-branches.

240 BMC Galatia, Cappadotia, Syria 184.
241 BMC Alexandria 156, A.G. 160.
242 BMC Alexandria 156, A.G. 160.
243 BMC Alexandria 165, A.G. 163.
244 BMC Alexandria 165, A.G. 163.
245 BMC Alexandria 165, A.G. 163.
246 BMC Alexandria 156, A.G. 170.

No.	Metal Size Weight	Axis	Denomination	Obverse	Reverse
A.D. 65/66, year 12					
247	AR 24.1 12.870	↑	Tetrdr.	ΝΕΡΩ[ΚΛΑΥΚΑΙΣΣΕ-ΒΓ]ΕΡ; bust of Nero r., radiate, wearing aegis.	ΑΥΤΟ [ΚΡΑ]; in front ⌊Ι[Β]; bust of Alexandria r., head covered with elephant's skin.
248	AR 24.2 13.380	↑	Tetrdr.	ΝΕΡΟΚΛΑΥΚ[ΑΙΣΣΕ-ΒΓΕΡ]. Similar.	Similar.
A.D. 66/67, year 13					
249	AR 22.3 12.700	↑	Tetrdr.	[ΝΕΡΩΚΛΑΥΚΑΙΣΣΕΒ]-ΓΕΡΑ; bust of Nero r., radiate, wearing aegis; in front, ⌊ΙΓ	[ΘΕΟΣ]ΣΕΒΑΣΤΟΣ; head of Augustus, radiate, r.
250	AR 24.5 13.010	↑	Tetrdr.	Similar, but ΝΕΡΩΚΛΑΥ-ΚΑΙΣΣΕ[ΒΓΕΡΑ].	Similar, but ΘΕΟ[Σ]ΣΕΒΑ ΣΤΟΣ.
251	AR 23.5 12.800	↑	Tetrdr.	[ΝΕΡΩΚΛΑΥΚΑΙ]ΣΣΕΒ-ΓΕΡΑΥ, in front, [⌊Ι]Γ; bust of Nero l., radiate, wearing aegis.	ΤΙΒΕΡΙΟΣ ΚΑΙΣ[ΑΡ]; head of Tiberius, laureate, r.
A.D. 67/68, year 14					
252	AR 25.0 12.910	↖	Tetrdr.	[ΝΕΡΩΚΛΑΥ] ΚΑΙΣΣΕΒ-ΓΕ[ΡΑΥ], in front, ⌊ΙΔ; bust of Nero l., radiate, wearing aegis.	ΗΡΑ ΑΡΓΕΙ[Α]; bust of Hera Argeia r., wearing stephane and veil.
253	AR 24.9 12.190	↖	Tetrdr.	[ΝΕΡΩΚΛΑΥΚΑΙ]ΣΣ ΕΒ-ΓΕΒΕΡΑΥ, in front, [⌊]ΙΔ; bust of Nero l., radiate wearing aegis.	[ΑΠΟΛ]ΛΩΝ ΠΥΘΕΙΟΣ bust of Apollon Pythios r., laureate; behind shoulder, quiver.

[247] BMC Alexandria 163, A.G. 172.
[248] BMC Alexandria 163, A.G. 172.
[249] BMC Alexandria 112, A.G. 177.
[250] BMC Alexandria 112, A.G. 177.
[251] BMC Alexandria 114, A.G. 187.
[252] BMC Alexandria 133, A.G. 199.
[253] BMC Alexandria 141, A.G. 197.

No.	Metal Size Weight	Axis	Deno- mina- tion	Obverse	Reverse

JUDEA

Antonius Felix, Procurator, A.D. 52–60
A.D. 58–59

No.	Metal Size Weight	Axis	Denomination	Obverse	Reverse
254	AE 16.2 2.100	↖	AE	[LЄKAICA] POC: palm branch.	In olive-wreath: NEP ωNO [c]
255	AE 16.1 2.580	↑	AE	Similar, but [LЄKAIC]-APOC.	Similar, but NEP ωNO C
256	AE 16.9 2.410	↑	AE	Similar.	Similar.
257	AE 15.4 1.950	↑	AE	Similar, but LЄ[KAICA]-POC.	Similar.
258	AE 16.3 2.350	↖	AE	Similar, but LЄ[KAIC]A-POC.	Similar, but NEP NOC [ω]NO C
259	AE 16.2 1.950	↑	AE	Similar, but LЄ[KAI-CAPO]C.	Similar, but [NEP ωNO] C
260	AE 16.3 2.810	↑	AE	Similar, but LЄKAICA-POC.	Similar, but NEP ωNO C.
261	AE 16.0 1.950	↑	AE	Similar, but [LЄ]KAICA-POC.	Similar, but [NEP ω]NO C
262	AE 16.1 2.430	↖	AE	Similar, but [LЄ]KAICA-POC.	Similar, but NEP ωNO ∩

[254] BMC Palestine 1–14.
[255] BMC Palestine 1–14.
[256] BMC Palestine 1–14.
[257] BMC Palestine 1–14.
[258] BMC Palestine 1–14.
[259] BMC Palestine 1–14.
[260] BMC Palestine 1–14.
[261] BMC Palestine 1–14.
[262] BMC Palestine 15–18.

No.	Metal Size Weight	Axis	Deno-mina-tion	Obverse	Reverse
263	AE 15.6 1.250	↖	AE	Similar, but LЄKAICAPO-[C].	Similar.
264	AE 15.4 1.370	↓	AE	Similar, but AIC OP. (!)	Similar.
265	AE 15.0 1.880	↓	AE	Similar, but LЄKAI[CA-PO] C.	Similar, but NEP ωNO [∩]
266	AE 17.1 3.050	↖	AE	Similar, but [L]ЄKA[IC]-APOC.	Similar, but NEP ωNO ∩
267	AE 15.9 2.300	↖	AE	Similar, but [LЄKAI]-CAPOC.	Similar.

Forgeries

Of coins issued by the mints of Rome and Lugdunum

c. A.D. 63–66

No.	Metal Size Weight	Axis	Denomination	Obverse	Reverse
268	Orch 25.3 8.280	↓	As	N[E]RO CLAVD CAESAR AVG GERMANIC; head of Nero, radiate, r.	PONTIF MAX TR POT IMP P P: Nero as Apollo Citharodeus advancing r. in the flowing robes, playing lyre held in l. hand.
269	AE 32.6 24.320	↓	S	NERO CLAVDIVS CAESAR AVG GERM TR P IMP P P; head of Nero, laureate, r.	ANNONA AVGVSTI CERES, S C in ex.; Ceres, veiled and draped, seated l., holding corn--ears and torch, her feet on stool; facing Annona, standing r., resting r. hand on hip l. holding cornucopiae between them, modius on altar; behind, ship's stern.

---

263 BMC Palestine 15–21.
264 BMC Palestine 15–21.
265 BMC Palestine 15–21.
266 BMC Palestine 15–21.
267 BMC Palestine 15–21.

No.	Metal Size Weight	Axis	Deno-mina-tion	Obverse	Reverse
270	AE 34.1 25.700	↙	S	Similar.	Similar.
271	Orch 35.1 24.370	↓	S	[NE]RO CLAVD CAESAR AVG GERM P M TR P IMP P P; bust of Nero, laureate, wearing aegis, r.	CONG [II DAT] POP, in ex., S C; Nero, seated l. on platform r., extended r. hand; behind him, prefect stg. facing; below in front, attendant stg. l. holding tessera to citizen stg. r.; in background, Minerva stg. facing, holding owl and spear.
272	AE 36.1 27.680	↓	S	NERO CLAVDIVS CAESAR AVG GER P M TR P IMP P P; head of Nero, laureate, r.	S – C to l. and r.; of Triumphal arch, surmounted by facing quadriga escorted on r. by Victory on l. by Pax; on l. side of arch in niche, figure of Mars standing facing, holding spear and shield.
273	AE 33.4 24.730	↓	S	NERO CLAVDIVS CAESAR AVG GER P M TR P IMP P P; head of Nero, laureate, r.	DECVRSIO, S – C to l. and r. of Nero pracing l. on horseback, holding in r. hand spear; beyond and behind him, mounted soldier pracing l. with vexillum held over r. shoulder.
274	AE 34.3 24.905	↓	S	[NERO CLA]VDIVS CAESAR AVG GER P M TR P [IMP P P]; head of Nero, laureate, r.	PACE P R TERRA [MARIQ] [P]ARTA IA[NVM CLVSIT]; S – C to l. and r. of front of the temple of Janus, with latticed window to l. and closed double doors to r.
275	Orch 32.8 20.010	↘	S	Similar, but NERO CLAVDIVS CAESAR AVG GER P M TR IMP II PP (!).	Similar, but PACE [P] R TE[RR]A MARIQ PARTA IANVM CLVSIT.
276	AE 34.8 23.350	↓	S	[NERO CL]AVD CAESAR AVG GE[RM P M TR P IMP P P]; head of Nero, laureate, r.	PORT AVG; view of the harbour of Ostia; at the top, pharos surmounted by statue of Neptune; at the bottom reclining figure of Tiber l., holding rudder and dolphin; in centre, five ships; the harbour is surrounded by pier on l., and break-water on r.

No.	Metal Size Weight	Axis	Deno-mina-tion	Obverse	Reverse
277	AE 35.0 24.770	↓	S	NERO CLAVD CAESAR AVG GER P M [TR P] IMP PP; head of Nero, laureate, l.,; globe at point of bust.	ROMA in ex., S – C to l. and r. of Roma, helmeted and in military dress, seated l. on cuirass, holding Victory in r. hand, l. resting on parazonium.
278	AE 28.0 12.395	↓	As	NERO CAESAR AVG GERM IMP: head of Nero, laureate, r.	S – C to l. and r. of Victory flying l., holding shield in both hands.
279	AE 27.8 10.020	↓	As	IMP NERO CAESAR AVG P M[AX TR P P P]; head of Nero, bare, r.	GENIO [AVGVSTI], S – C to l. and r. of Genius standing half-left, sacrificing from patera over altar with r. hand, in r. holding cornucopiae.
280	Orch 23.4 5.150	↓	As	Similer, but trace of legend.	Similar, but [GENIO] AVGVSTI.

Of coin issued by the eastern mint

No.	Metal Size Weight	Axis	Deno-mina-tion	Obverse	Reverse
281	AE 25.2 14.270	↓	AE	NHPO ... MOKT; head of Nero (?), laureate, r.	OKTAYIA ΣΕΒΑΣΤΗ; bust of Octavia, draped, r.

GALBA (A.D. 68–69)

Imperial Issues

Mint of Rome
c. July 68 – January 69

No.	Metal Size Weight	Axis	Deno-mina-tion	Obverse	Reverse
282	AR 18.1 3.100	↓	D	IMP SER GALBA [AVG]; head of Galba, bare, r.	S P Q R OB C S in oak-wreath.
283	AR 18.0 3.270	↓	D	Similar, but IMP SER GALBA AVG.	Similar.
284	AR 17.6 3.160	↓	D	Similar, but [IMP] SER GALBA [AVG].	Similar.

[282] RICr 167, RIC 20, BMC 34.
[283] RICr 167, RIC 20, BMC 34.
[284] RICr 167, RIC 20, BMC 34.

No.	Metal Size Weight	Axis	Denomination	Obverse	Reverse
285	AR 19.1 2.770	↓	D	IMP SER GALB[A CAE] SAR AVG; bust of Galba, draped, r., head laureate.	VICTORIA P R; Victory, draped, standing l. on globe, holding wreath in r. hand, in l. palm.
286	AR 17.4 3.100	↘	D	[IMP SER] GALBA CAESAR AVG P [M]; head of Galba, laureate, r.	Similar.

AES

A.D. 68

No.	Metal Size Weight	Axis	Denomination	Obverse	Reverse
287	AE 32.6 25.030	↓	S	[IMP SER GAL]BA CAESAR AVG [TR P]; head of Galba, laureate, r.	CON[CORD AVG]; S – C to l. and r. of Concordia, draped, seated l. on throne, holding in r. hand olive-branch, in l. transverse sceptre.
288	AE 27.6 10.870	↓	As	IMP SER GALBA CAES AVG P M TR P; head of Galba, bare, r.	LIBERTAS PVBLICA, S – C to l. and r. of Libertas, draped, standing l., holding pileus in r. hand, in l. vertcal rod.
289	AE 26.7 8.270	↓	As	Similar.	Similar.

c. October 68

No.	Metal Size Weight	Axis	Denomination	Obverse	Reverse
290	AE 35.8 26.260	↓	S	SER GALBA IMP CAESAR AVG TR P; head of Galba, laureate, l.	LIBERTAS PVBLICA, S – C to l. and r. of Libertas, draped, standing l., holding pileus in r. hand, in l., vertical rod.
291	AE 34.5 22.820	↓	S	SER GALBA IMP [CAESAR AVG T]R P; head of Galba, laureate, r.	S P Q R OB CIV SER in oak-wreath.

---

[285] RICr 217, RIC 24, BMC 49.
[286] RICr 234, RIC 24.
[287] RICr 344, RIC 28, BMC 61.
[288] RIC 60, BMC 147.
[289] RIC 60, BMC 147.
[290] RICr 389, RIC 35, BMC 68.
[291] RICr 404, RIC 50, BMC 111.

No.	Metal Size Weight	Axis	Deno-mina-tion	Obverse	Reverse

HYBRID

No.	Metal Size Weight	Axis	Deno-mina-tion	Obverse	Reverse
292	AE 35.4 26.400	↓	S	SER GALBA IMP CAES AVG; bust of Galba, draped, r., head laureate.	NERO CLAVDIVS DRVSVS GERMAN IMP. S – C to l. and r. of triumphal arch surmounted by equestrian statue r. between trophies.

Provincial Issues

AEGYPTUS

Mint of Aleksandria
A.D. 68/69, year 2

No.	Metal Size Weight	Axis	Deno-mina-tion	Obverse	Reverse
293	AR 24.2 13.550	↗	Tetrdr.	ΣΕΡΟVΙΓΑΛΒ[ΑΑVΤΟ-ΚΑΙ ΣΣΕΒΑ; head of Galba, laureate, r.; in front, ∟B.	ΕΛ[ΕV ΘΕΡΙΑ]; Eleuteria, standing l., resting on column, holding wreath in r. hand in l., sceptra; in front, simpulum.

Forgeries

Of coins issued by the mint of Rome
c. A.D. 68

No.	Metal Size Weight	Axis	Deno-mina-tion	Obverse	Reverse
294	Orch 35.5 23.650	↓	S	IMP [SER S]VLP GALBA CAES AVG TR P; bust of Galba, draped, r., head laureate.	LIBE[RTAS PV]BLICA, S – C to l. and r. of Libertas, draped, standing l., holding pileus in r. hand, in l., vertical rod.
295	AE 33.7 23.500	↓	S	SER [GAL]BA IMP CAES AVG; bust of Galba, draped, r., head laureate.	[S P Q R] OB CIV SER, in oak-wreath
296	AE 33.6 25.050	↓	S	SER GALBA [I]MP CAES [AV]G TR P; head of Galba, laureate, r.	Similar, but S P Q R OB CIV SER.

---

292 Öbv. RICr 256; Rv. (Claudius) RICr 98, RIC 62.
293 BMC Alexandria 193, A.G. 233.
296 Coin perforated.

No.	Metal Size Weight	Axis	Denomination	Obverse	Reverse

OTHO (15 I – 25 IV 69)

Imperial Issues

15 January – mid-April 69

No.	Metal Size Weight	Axis	Denomination	Obverse	Reverse
297	AR 17.7 2.610	↓	D	IMP OTHO [CAESAR AVG] TR P; head of Otho, bare, r.	[S]ECVRITAS P R; Securitas, draped, standing l., holding wreath in r. hand, in l., sceptre.

Doubtful

No.	Metal Size Weight	Axis	Denomination	Obverse	Reverse
298	AR 19.2 3.190	↓	D	IMP OTHO CAESAR AVG TR P; head of Otho, bare, r.	PAX ORBIS TERRARVM; Pax, draped, standing l., holding branch in r. hand, in l., caduceus.

Forgery

No.	Metal Size Weight	Axis	Denomination	Obverse	Reverse
299	AR 17.9 3.010	↘	D	IMP M OTHO CAESAR AVG TR P; head of Otho, bare, r.	SECVRITAS P R; Securitas, draped, standing l., holding wreath in r. hand, in l., sceptre.

VITELLIVS (2 I – 20 XII 69)

Imperial Issues

Mint of Rome

c. Late April – 20 December 69

No.	Metal Size Weight	Axis	Denomination	Obverse	Reverse
300	AR 18.4 2.320	↓	D	[A V]ITELLIVS GERMANICVS IMP; head of Vitellius, bare, r.	Fides [E]XFERCITVVS; clasped hands.
301	AR 18.5 3.000	↓	D	[A VITEL]LIVS GERMAN IMP TR P; head of Vitellius, laureate, r.	S P Q R OB C. S. in oak-wreath.
302	AR 20.0 3.210	↙	D	[A VITELLIVS] GERM IMP AVG TR P; head of Vitellius, laureate, r.	CONCORDIA P R; Concordia, draped, seated l. holding patera in r. hand, in l. cornucopia.

[297] RICr 10, RIC 12, BMC 19.
[298] RICr 5, RIC 3, BMC 4 – but head l.
[300] RICr 67, RIC 3, BMC 2.
[301] RICr 83, RIC 22, BMC 15.
[302] RICr 90, RIC 2, BMC 20.

No.	Metal Size Weight	Axis	Denomination	Obverse	Reverse
303	AR 18.1 2.805	↓	D	Similar, but A [VITE]LLIVS GERM IMP AVG [TR P].	Similar, but CONCO[RDIA P R].
304	AR 18.3 3.055	↓	D	[A] VITELLIVS GERM IMP AVG TR P; head of Vitellius, laureate, r.	LIBER[TAS] RESTITVTA; Libertas, draped, standing facing, head r., holding pileus in r. hand, in l. long rod.

HYBRID

No.	Metal Size Weight	Axis	Denomination	Obverse	Reverse
305	AR 18.0 2.870	↓	D	A VITELLIVS GERMAN IMP TR P; head of Vitellius, bare, r.	CONCORDIA P R; Concordia, dr., seated l., holding patera in r. hand, in l. cornucopia.

Forgeries

No.	Metal Size Weight	Axis	Denomination	Obverse	Reverse
306	AE 31.4 11.750	↓	S	A VITELLIVS GERMANICVS IMP AVG P M TR P; bust of Vitelius, draped, head laureate	HONOS ET VIRTVS; S C in ex.; Honos on l. and Virtus on r., standing each other; Honos holding cornucopia in l. hand in r. long sceptre; Virtus holding parazonium on knee in r. hand in l. spear, r. foot on helmet.
307	AE 34.9 22.120	↓	S	A VITELLIVS GERMAN IMP AVG P M P P; bust of Vitellius, draped, head laureate, r.	LIBERTAS RESTITVTA; S – C to l. and r. of Libertas, draped, standing l., holding pileus in r. hand, in l. long rod.

VESPASIAN (A.D. 69–79)

Imperial Issues

Mint of Rome
A.D. 69–71

No.	Metal Size Weight	Axis	Denomination	Obverse	Reverse
308	AR 18.7 2.390	↓	D	IMP CAESAR VESPASIA[NVS AVG]; head of Vespasian, laureate, r.	[COS ITE]R F[ORT RED]; Fortune, draped, standing l., setting r. hand on prow, in l. holding cornucopia.

[303] RICr 90, RIC 2, BMC 20.
[304] RICr 105, RIC 18, BMC 31.
[305] RICr p. 273.
[308] RIC 4, BMC 7.

No.	Metal Size Weight	Axis	Denomination	Obverse	Reverse
309	AR 18.9 3.095	↓	D	Similar, but IMP CAESAR VES[PASIA]NVS AVG.	Similar, but COS ITER [FO]-RT RED.
310	AR 18.3 3.230	↓	D	[IMP CAE]SAR VESPASIANVS AVG; head of Vespasian, laureate, r.	COS ITER TR POT: Pax, seated l., holding branch in extending r. hand, in l., caduceus.
311	AR 17.1 3.180	↙	D	Similar, but IMP CAESAR VESPASIANVS AVG.	Similar.
312	AR 17.6 3.010	↘	D	Similar, but [IMP CAES]AR VESPASIANV[S AVG].	Similar, but COS ITER [TR] POT.
313	AR 16.6 3.070	↓	D	[IMP CAESAR] VESPASIANVS AVG; head of Vespasian, laureate, r.	IVDE[A]; Judea, seated r. on ground, mourning; behind her, trophy.
A.D. 70–72					
314	AR 17.9 2.870	↓	D	[IMP] CAES VESP AVG P M. Head of Vespasian, laureate, r.	AVGV[R] TRI P[OT]. Simpulum, aspergillum, jug and lituus.
315	AR 17.1 2.870	↓	D	Similar, but [IMP CAES] VESP AV[G P M].	Similar, but AVGVR TR[I] POT.
316	AR 16.1 3.100	↓	D	Similar, but [IMP CAES] VESP AVG P M.	Similar, but [A]VGV[R] [T]-RI POT.
317	AR 17.2 3.295	↓	D	Similar, but [IMP CAE]S VESP AVG [P M].	Similar, but AVGV[R] TRI POT.

[309] RIC 4, BMC 7.
[310] RIC 10, BMC 26.
[311] RIC 10, BMC 26.
[312] RIC 10, BMC 26.
[313] RIC 15, BMC 35.
[314] RIC 30, BMC 48.
[315] RIC 30, BMC 48.
[316] RIC 30, BMC 48.
[317] RIC 30, BMC 48.

No.	Metal Size Weight	Axis	Deno- mina- tion	Obverse	Reverse
318	AR 17.6 2.650	↓	D	IMP CAES [VESP AVG P M]. Head of Vespasian, laureate, r.	PON MA[X], across field. Vesta, seated l., holding simpulum in extended r. hand.
319	AR 16.5 2.550	↓	D	Similar, but IMP [CAES VESP AVG P M].	Similar, but TRI POT across field.
320	AR 18.1 3.050	↓	D	IMP CAES VESP [AVG] P M. Head of Vespasian, laureate, r.	TRI POT [II] COS III P P. Pax seated l., holding branch in extended r. hand, in l. caduceus.
A.D. 72–73					
321	AR 17.4 3.090	↓	D	[IMP CA]ES VESP AVG P M [COS IIII]. Head of Vespasian, laureate r.	[A]VGV[R] TRI POT. Simpulum, aspergillum, jug and lituus.
322	AR 17.3 3.150	↙	D	Similar, but [IMP CA]ES VESP AVG P M COS IIII.	Similar, but AVGVR TRI PO[T]
323	AR 18.1 3.010	↓	D	Similar, but IMP [CAES VESP AV]G P M COS IIII.	Similar, but AVGVR TRI POT.
324	AR 17.1 2.950	↓	D	[IMP CAES] VESP AVG P M CO[S IIII]. Head of Vespasian, laureate, r.	[VESTA]. Vesta, standing l., holding simpulum in r. hand, in l. sceptre.
325	AR 17.2 1.880	↓	Q	IMP CAES VESP AVG P M COS IIII. Head of Vespasian, laureate, r.	[VI]CTORIA [AVGVSTI]. Victoria advancing r., holding palm and about to place wreath on trophy.

[318] RIC 36, BMC 55.
[319] RIC 37, BMC 57; coin perforated.
[320] RIC 39, BMC 61.
[321] RIC 42, BMC 64.
[322] RIC 42, BMC 64.
[323] RIC 42, BMC 64.
[324] RIC 50, BMC 71.
[325] RIC 52, BMC 74.

No.	Metal Size Weight	Axis	Denomination	Obverse	Reverse
A.D. 73					
326	AR 19.2 3.385	↑	D	IMP CAES VESP AVG CENS. (Starting r., autwardly). Head of Vespasian, laureate, r.	PONTIF MAXIM. Vespasian, seated r., holding branch in extended l. hand, in r. sceptre.
327	AR 18.9 2.400	↖	D	Similar.	Similar, but [PONTIF] MAXIM.
328	AR 18.5 3.235	↑	D	Similar, but IMP CAES VESP AVG [CENS].	Similar, but PONTIF [MAXIM].
329	AR 18.9 3.205	↑	D	Similar, but IMP CAES VESP AVG CENS.	Similar, but PONTIF MAXIM.
330	AR 18.4 3.320	↓	D	IMP CAES VESP AVG CEN, starting l. Head of Vespasian, laureate, r.	SALV[S] AVG. Salus seated l., holding patera in exteding r. hand.
A.D. 74					
331	AR 18.3 3.380	↓	D	IMP CAESAR VESPASIANVS AVG, starting r. Head of Vespasian, laureate, r.	PON MAX TR P COS V, starting r. Winged caduceus.
332	AR 17.2 2.690	↘	D	Similar.	Similar.
333	AR 18.4 3.400	↓	D	IMP CAESAR VESP[ASIANVS AVG], starting r. Head of Vespasian, laureate, r.	PON MAX TR P COS V, starring r. Vespasian, seated r., holding branch in extending l. hand, in r. sceptre.
334	AR 19.0 3.150	↓	D	Similar, but IMP [CAESAR] VESPASIANVS AVG.	Similar, but [P]ON MAX TR P COS V.

[326] RIC 65, BMC 98.
[327] RIC 65, BMC 98.
[328] RIC 65, BMC 98.
[329] RIC 65, BMC 98.
[330] RIC 67, BMC 105.
[331] RIC 75, BMC 138.
[332] RIC 75, BMC 138.
[333] RIC 77, BMC 135.
[334] RIC 77, BMC 135.

No.	Metal Size Weight	Axis	Deno-mina-tion	Obverse	Reverse
335	AR 18.7 2.870	↓	D	Smilar, but IMP CAESAR VESPASIAN[VS AVG].	Similar, but PON MAX [TR] P COS [V].
336	AR 18.6 3.200	↓	D	Similar, but [IMP CAE-SAR] VESPASIANVS AVG.	Similar, but [PON MAX] TR P COS V.
A.D. 75					
337	AR 19.6 3.230	↓	D	[I]MP CAESAR VES-P[ASIAN VS AVG]. Head of Vespasian, lau-reate, r.	[C]OS [VI]. Eagle stand-ing on cippus, head to l.
338	AR 18.5 3.230	↙	D	Similar, but [IMP CAE]-SAR VESPASIANVS AV[G].	Similar, but [C]OS VI.
339	AR 17.7 3.250	↓	D	IMP CAESAR VESPA-S[IANVS AVG]. Head of Vespasianus, laureate, r.	PON MAX TR R P COS VI. Pax, seated l., holding branch in extending r. hand.
340	AR 19.0 2.885	↓	D	IMP CAESAR VESPASIA-NVS AVG. Similar.	Similar.
341	AR 17.2 2.930	↘	D	Similar, but [IMP CAE-SAR] VESPASIANVS [AVG].	Similar, but PON MAX [TR P] COS VI.
A.D. 76					
342	AR 18.6 3.025	↙	D	[IMP CAESAR] VESPA-SIA NVS AVG, starting r. Head of Vespasian, laurea-te, r.	COS VII. Cow, walking r.
343	AR 16.7 2.025	↓	D	Similar.	Similar.

335 RIC 77, BMC 135.
336 RIC 77, BMC 135.
337 RIC 89, BMC p. 30.
338 RIC 89, BMC p. 30.
339 RIC 90, BMC 161.
340 RIC 90, BMC 161.
341 RIC 90, BMC 161.
342 RIC 96, BMC 177.
343 RIC 96, BMC 177.

No.	Metal Size Weight	Axis	Denomination	Obverse	Reverse
A.D. 77–78					
344	AR 18.1 3.010	↓	D	[IMP] CAESAR [VES]PASIANVS AVG, starting r. Head of Vespasian, laureate, r.	COS VIII. Yoke of oxen, l.
345	AR 18.6 2.935	↓	D	CAESAR [VESPASI]ANVS AV[G], starting r. Head of Vespasian, laureate, r.	IMP X[IX]. Sow l. with three young.
346	AR 17.6 2.900	↙	D	Similar, but CAESAR VESPASIANVS AVG.	IMP XIX to l. and. r. Modius and corn-ears.
A.D. 79					
347	AR 18.1 3.485	↓	D	IMP CAESAR VESPASIANVS AVG, starting r. Head of Vespasian, laureate, r.	TR POT X COS VIIII. Ceres, seated l., holding corn-ears in extending r. hand in l., torch.
348	AR 17.6 2.750	↓	D	[IMP CAE]SAR VESPASIA NV S AVG, starting r. Head of Vespasian, laureate, r.	TR PO[T X COS VIIII]. Radiate figure, standing facing on rostral column, holding spear in r. hand, in l. parazonium.
A.D. 75–79. Undated					
349	AR 18.4 3.220	↓	D	[IMP C]AESAR VESPASIANVS AVG, starting r. Head of Vespasian, laureate, r.	[I]OVIS CVS[TOS]. Jupiter, standing l., sacrificing out of patera over altar and holding sceptre in l. hand.
350	AR 19.2 2.200	↓	D	Similar, but [IMP CAESAR] VESPASIANVS AVG.	Similar, but [IO]VIS CV STOS.
351	AR 18.4 3.230	↓	D	CAESAR VESPASIANVS AVG, starting r. Head of Vespasian, laureate, r.	ANNONA AVG: Annona, seated l., feet on stool, holding on lap a sack of corn-ears open, the ties, looped at one end, in her hands.

[344] RIC 107, BMC 206.
[345] RIC 109, BMC 212.
[346] RIC 110, BMC 216.
[347] RIC 113, BMC 243.
[348] RIC 119, BMC 253.
[349] RIC 124a, BMC 276.
[350] RIC 124a, BMC 276.
[351] RIC 131b, BMC 295.

No.	Metal Size Weight	Axis	Denomination	Obverse	Reverse
352	AR 18.4 2.420	↓	D	Similar, but [CAESAR] VESPASIANVS [AVG].	Similar, but ANNONA [AVG].

TITUS (striking under Vespasian)

Mint of Rome
A.D. 74

No.	Metal Size Weight	Axis	Denomination	Obverse	Reverse
353	AR 18.1 2.880	↓	D	T CAESAR IMP VES[PASIAN], starting r.; head of Titus, laureate, r.	PONTIF TR P COS [III], starting r.; Titus seated r., holding branch in extending r. hand, in l. sceptre.

A.D. 75–79

No.	Metal Size Weight	Axis	Denomination	Obverse	Reverse
354	AR 18.9 2.790	↓	D	T [CA]ESAR IMP VESPASIANVS, starting r.; head of Titus, laureate, r.	[IO]VI[S] CVSTOS; Jupiter standing l., sacrificing out of patera over altar and holding sceptre.

A.D. 78/79

No.	Metal Size Weight	Axis	Denomination	Obverse	Reverse
355	AR 19.5 3.070	↓	D	T CAESAR VESPASIANVS, starting r.; head of Titus, laureate, r.	ANNON[A A]VG; Annona seated l., holding corn-ears (?) in r. hand.

DOMITIAN (striking under Vespasian)

Mint of Rome
A.D. 76

No.	Metal Size Weight	Axis	Denomination	Obverse	Reverse
356	AR 18.5 3.200	↓	D	CAESAR AVG F DOMITIANVS, starting r.; head of Domitian, laureate, r.	COS IIII; Pegasus walking r.
357	AR 18.8 3.020	↘	D	Similar, but [CAES]AR AVG [F DOMI]TIANVS.	Similar.

---

352 RIC 131b, BMC 295.
353 RIC 174, BMC 150.
354 RIC 211, BMC 305.
355 RIC 218, BMC 319.
356 RIC 238, BMC 193.
357 RIC 238, BMC 193.

No.	Metal Size Weight	Axis	Denomination	Obverse	Reverse
358	AR 18.6 2.700	↓	D	Similar, but CAESAR [AVG F DOMITIA]NVS.	Similar, but [COS IIII].
A.D. 77–78					
359	AR 19.4 2.780	↓	D	CAESAR AVG F DOMITIANVS, starting r.; head of Domitian, laureate, r.	CO[S V]; she-wolf and twins; in exergue, boat.
360	AR 19.5 3.010	→	D	Simmilar, but [CAE]SAR AVG F DOMITIANVS.	COS V; horseman helmeted r., hand raised.

AES

Mint of Rome
A.D. 71

No.	Metal Size Weight	Axis	Denomination	Obverse	Reverse
361	AE 32.0 23.750	↓		IMP [CAES VES]PAS AVG P M TR P P P COS III; head of Vespasian, laureate, r.	IVDE[A CAPTA]; S C in ex.; Jewess ·ated r. under palm-tree, mourning; behind palm, Vespasian standing r., holding spear and parazonium.
362	AE 33.0 20.890	↓		IMP CAES VESPAS AVG P M TR P P P COS III; head of Vespasian, laureate, r.	PAX [AVGVSTI]; S – C to l. and r. of Pax standing l. holding branch in extending r. hand, in l. cornucopiae.
363	AE 33.7 25.650	↓	S	Similar, but IMP CAES VESPAS AVG [P M TR P] P P COS III.	Similar, but PAX AVGVSTI.
364	AE 32.3 25.560	↘	S	Similar, but IMP CAES VESPAS AVG P M TR P P P COS III.	Similar, but [PAX A]VGVSTI.
365	AE 31.2 24.200	↓	S	Similar.	Similar, but [PAX] AVGVSTI.

358 RIC 238, BMC 193.
359 RIC 241, BMC 241.
360 RIC 242, BMC 235.
361 RIC 427, BMC 543.
362 RIC 437, BMC 554.
363 RIC 437, BMC 554.
364 RIC 437, BMC 554.
365 RIC 437, BMC 554.

No.	Metal Size Weight	Axis	Denomination	Obverse	Reverse
366	AE 34.3 23.885	↓	S	IMP CAES VESPASIAN AVG P M TR P P P COS III; head of Vespasian, laureate, r.	ROMA, S – C to l. and r. of Roma, standing l. holding Victory in extending r. hand, in l. spear.
367	AE 33.9 25.185	↓	S	Similar, but IMP CAES VESPASIAN AVG P M TR P [P P] COS [III].	Similar.
368	AE 32.1 20.600	↓	S	IMP [CAES] VESPAS AVG P M TR P P P COS III; head of Vespasian, laureate, r.	SA[LVS] AVGVSTA, S C in ex.; Salus seated l., holding patera in extending r. hand in l. sceptre.
369	AE 27.1 12.875	↓	Dp	[IMP CAES] VESPASIAN AVG [COS III]; head of Vespasian, radiate, r.	CONCORDIA [AVG]. [S C] in ex. Concordia seated l., sacrificing out over altar and holding cornucopiae.
370	AE 27.9 11.710	↓	Dp	IMP CAES VESPASIAN [AVG COS III]; head of Vespasian, radiate, r.	ROM[A], in ex. S – C to l., and r. Roma seated l., holding wreath in extended r. hand, l. resting on parazonium at side.
371	AE 26.2 12.080	↓	Dp	Similar, but IMP CAES VESPASIAN AVG COS III.	Similar, but ROMA.
372	AE 28.8 13.950	↓	Dp	IMP CAES VESPASIAN AVG COS [III]; head of Vespasian, radiate, r.	SECVRI[TAS AVGVSTI]. S C in ex. Securitas seated r., resting head on r. hand and holding sceptre in l.; in front altar.
373	AE 24.7 9.470	↓	As	IMP CAES VESPASIAN AVG COS III; head of Vespasian, laureate, l.	[AEQVITAS] AVGVSTI. S – C to l. and r. Aequitas standing l., holding scales in extending r. hand and rod in l.

366 RIC 443, BMC 560.
367 RIC 443, BMC 560.
368 RIC 460, BMC 574.
369 RIC 470, BMC 588.
370 RIC 476, BMC 591.
371 RIC 476, BMC 591.
372 RIC 479, BMC 595+.
373 RIC 485, BMC 600.

No.	Metal Size Weight	Axis	Denomination	Obverse	Reverse
374	AE 26.3 11.330	↓	As	IMP CAES VESPASIAN AVG COS III; head of Vespasian, laureate, l.	VICTORIA NAVALIS. S – C to l. and r. Victory standing r. on prow, holding wreath in exteding r. hand, in l. palm.
375	AE 26.7 9.910	↓	As	Similar.	Similar.
376	AE 27.5 12.090	↓	As	IMP CAES VASPASIAN AVG COS [III]; head of Vespasian, laureate, r.	S – C to l. and r. of eagle standing on globe, head r.
A.D. 72–73					
377	AE 25.5 10.380	↘	As	IMP CAES VESPASIAN AVG P P COS IIII; head of Vespasian, laureate, r.	AEQVITAS AVGVSTI; S – C to l. and r. of Aequitas standing l., holding scales in extending r. hand, in l. rod.
A.D. 73					
378	AE 27.0 12.910	↓	Dp	[IMP] CAES VESP AVG P M T P COS IIII CENS; head of Vespasian, radiate, r.	FELICITAS PVBLICA; S – C to l. and r. of Felicitas standing l., holding caduceus in r. hand, in l. cornucopia.
379	AE 26.1 10.025	↓	Dp	Similar, but IMP CAES VESP AVG P M T P [COS IIII CENS].	Similar, but FELI [CITAS PV-BLIC]A.
380	AE 27.9 8.930	↘	As	[IMP CAE]S VESP AVG [P M T P COS IIII] CENS; head of Vespasian, laureate, r.	S – C to l. and r. of Spes advancing l., holding flower in extending r. hand.
A.D. 74					
381	AE 26.4 10.700	↓	Dp	IMP CAES VESP AVG P M T P COS V CENS; head of Vespasian, radiate, r.	FELICITAS PVBLICA, S – C to l. and r. of Felicitas standing l., holding caduceus in r. hand, in l. cornucopia.

[374] RIC 503, BMC 616 – but head r.
[375] RIC 503, BMC 616 – but head r.
[376] RIC 497, BMC 612.
[377] RIC 527, BMC 625.
[378] RIC 539a, BMC 661, head l.
[379] RIC 539a, BMC 661, head l.
[380] RIC 545, BMC 663^{+}.
[381] RIC 554, BMC 696.

No.	Metal Size Weight	Axis	Denomination	Obverse	Reverse
382	AE 28.0 11.230	↓	Dp	Similar, but IMP CAES VESP AVG P M T P COS V [CENS].	Similar, but FELICITAS [PV-BLICA].
383	AE 26.0 12.250	↓	Dp	Similar.	Similar, but FELICITAS [P]V-BLICA.
384	AE 26.7 9.985	↓	As	[IMP] CAESAR VESP AVG COS V CENS; head of Vespasian, laureate, r.	PAX AV[GVST]; S – C to l. and r. of Pax standing l., learing on cippus, holding caduceus and branch.
385	AE 26.5 9.925	↓	As	Similar, but [IMP CAES] VESP AVG P [M T P] COS [V CENS].	Similar, but [PAX] AVGVST.
A.D. 75					
386	AE 27.6 10.700	↓	Dp	IMP CAES VESP AVG P M T P COS VI; head of Vespasian, radiate, r.	FELICI[TAS PV]BL[I]CA; S – C to l. and r. of Felicitas standing l., holding caduceus in r. hand, in l. cornucopia.
387	AE 14.4 3.000	↓	Quad	[IMP] VESPASIAN AVG; rudder on globe.	P M TR [P] P P COS VI; winged caduceus.
A.D. 76					
388	AE 26.5 11.060	↓	Dp	IMP CAES VESP AVG P M T P COS VII; head of Vespasian, radiate, r.	FELICITAS PVBLICA; S – C to l. and r. of Felicitas, standing l., holding caduceus in r. hand, in l. cornucopia.
389	AE 27.3 12.000	↓	Dp	Similar.	Similar, but FELICITAS [PV]-BLICA.

382 RIC 554, BMC 696.
383 RIC 554, BMC 696.
384 RIC 559b, BMC 702+.
385 RIC 559b, BMC 702+.
386 RIC 567, BMC 714.
387 RIC 569, BMC 715.
388 RIC 578, BMC 723.
389 RIC 578, BMC 723.

No.	Metal Size Weight	Axis	Denomination	Obverse	Reverse
390	AE 25.8 10.330	↓	Dp	Similar.	Similar, but FELICITAS [PV-BLI]CA.
391	AE 27.8 10.270	↓	Dp	Similar, but IMP CAES [VES]P AVG P M T P COS VII.	Similar, but FELICI[TA]S PV-BLICA.

TITUS (striking under Vespasian)

A.D. 72

No.	Metal Size Weight	Axis	Denomination	Obverse	Reverse
392	AE 30.8 14.600	↙	S	[T CAES] VESPA-SIAN IMP PON TR POT [COS II]; head of Titus, laureate, r.	[CAE]SAR DOMIT[IAN] COS DES II]; S – C to l. and r. Domitian, in military dress, on horse riding l., holding sceptre in l. hand.

A.D. 73

No.	Metal Size Weight	Axis	Denomination	Obverse	Reverse
393	AE 27.4 9.950	↓	As	[T CAE]S IMP PON TR P COS II CENS; head of Titus, laureate, r.	PAX AVG[VST]; S – C to l. snd r. Pax standing l., leaning on column, holding caduceus in extending r. hand, in l., branch.

DOMITIAN (striking under Vespasian)

A.D. 73

No.	Metal Size Weight	Axis	Denomination	Obverse	Reverse
394	AE 28.6 8.880	↓	As	CAESAR AVG F DOMI-TIAN COS II; head of Do-mitian, laureate, l.	PAX AVGVST; S – C to l. and r. Pax standing l. leaning on column, holding caduceus in extending r. hand, in l., branch.

HYBRIDS

Ob. of Vespasian

No.	Metal Size Weight	Axis	Denomination	Obverse	Reverse
395	AE 27.8 10.800	↓	As	IMP CAES VESPASIAN AVG COS IIII; head of Ves-pasian, laureate, r.	VICTORIA NAVALIS; S – C to l. and r. Victory standing r. on prow, holding wreath in extending r. hand, in l. palm.

[390] RIC 578, BMC 723.
[391] RIC 578, BMC 723.
[392] RIC 605, BMC 628.
[393] RIC 654, BMC 672⁺.
[394] RIC 696, BMC 684.
[395] Obv.: RIC 528a; Rv.: RIC 503.

No.	Metal Size Weight	Axis	Deno-mina-tion	Obverse	Reverse
396	AE 27.4 9.395	↓	As	IMP CAESAR VESPA-SIAN COS VIII; head of Vespasian, laureate, l.	AE[QVITAS] AVGVSTI; S – C to l. and r. Aequitas standing l., holding seales in r. hand, in l., rod.

Mint of Lugdunum
A.D. 77–78

No.	Metal Size Weight	Axis	Deno-mina-tion	Obverse	Reverse
397	AE 28.0 12.690	↓	Dp	[IMP] CAES] VESPA-SIAN AVG COS [VIII P P]; head of Vespasian, laureate, r.	FORTV[NAE REDV]CI; S – C to l. and r. Fortune holding rudder on globe in r. hand, in l., cornucopia.

TITUS (striking under Vespasian)

A.D. 72

No.	Metal Size Weight	Axis	Deno-mina-tion	Obverse	Reverse
398	AE 32.7 25.585	↓	S	T [CAE]SAR VESPASIAN IMP PON TR P[OT CO]S II; head of Titus, laureate, r.	S – C to l. and r. Mars advancing r., holding transverse spear in r. hand and trophy over l. shoulder.
399	AE 31.3 23.685	↓	S	Similar, but [T] CAESAR VESPASIAN IMP PON TR POT [COS II].	Similar, but S –C.

HYBRID

Ob. of Vespasian

No.	Metal Size Weight	Axis	Deno-mina-tion	Obverse	Reverse
400	AE 27.4 10.360	↓	Dp	[IMP CAESAR] VESPA-SIAN AVG COS IIII; head of Vespasian, radiate, r.	[VICTORIA] AVGVST; S – C to l. and r. Victoria flying l., r. leg advanced, holding wreath in extending r. hand, in l. palm.

Mint of Commagene
A.D. 74

No.	Metal Size Weight	Axis	Deno-mina-tion	Obverse	Reverse
401	AE 28.0 12.185	↓	Dp	IMP CAESAR VESPA-SIAN VS AVG; head of Vespasian, laureate, r.	[PON] MAX TR POT [P P COS] V CENS; winged caduceus between crossed cornucopiae.

[396] Obv.: RIC 597; Rv.: RIC 581.
[397] RIC 754, BMC 833.
[398] RIC 611, BMC 825B.
[399] RIC 611, BMC 825B.
[400] Obv.: RIC 739; Rv.: Nero, RICr type 31, RIC 301.
[401] RIC 798a, BMC 886.

No.	Metal Size Weight	Axis	Denomination	Obverse	Reverse
402	AE 27.9 10.980	↙	Dp	Similar, but IMP CAESAR VESPASIANVS AVG.	Similar, but PON MAX TR POT [P P COS] V CENS.

TITUS (striking under Vespasian)

A.D. 74

No.	Metal Size Weight	Axis	Denomination	Obverse	Reverse
403	AE 27.0 13.860	↓	Dp	T CAESAR IMP PONT; head of Titus, laureate, r.	TR POT COS III CENSOR; winged caduceus between crossed cornucopiae.
404	AE 27.2 11.200	↓	Dp	Similar, but T CAESAR IMP PO[NT].	Similar, but [TR POT COS] III CENSOR.

FORGERIES

Of coins issued by the mint of Rome

No.	Metal Size Weight	Axis	Denomination	Obverse	Reverse
405	AE 32.7 17.400	↓	S	IMP CAES VESPASIAN AVG P M TR P P P COS II; head of Vespasian, laureate, r.	ROMA RESVRGES; S C in ex.; Vespasian standing l., extending r. hand to raise up Roma kneeling r.; in background Minerva standing r.
406	AE 32.3 22.785	↓	S	IMP [CAES] VESPAS AVG P M TR P P P COS III; head of Vespasian, laureate, r.	[VICTORIA] AVGVSTI; S C in ex; Victory standing r., l. foot on helmet, writing OB CIV SER on shield hung on palm-tree.
407	AE 31.9 22.435	↓	S	IMP CAES VESPAS AVG P M TR P P COS III; head of Vespasian, laureate, r.	P[AX AVGVSTI] S – C to l. and r. Pax standing l., holding branch in extending r. hand, in l. cornucopia.
408	AE 26.4 12.990	↓	Dp	IMP CAES VESPASIAN AVG COS III; head of Vespasian, radiate, r.	[CO]NCORDIA [AVG]; S C in ex.; Concordia seated l., sacrificing out of patera over altar and holding cornucopia.

---

[402] RIC 798a, BMC 886.
[403] RIC 813a, BMC 891.
[404] RIC 813a, BMC 891.

No.	Metal Size Weight	Axis	Denomination	Obverse	Reverse
409	AE 30.160 11.160	↓	Dp	IMP CAES VESPASIAN AVG CO [S III]; head of Vespasian, radiate, r.	ROMA in ex.; S – C to l. and r. Roma seated l., holding wreath in extending r. hand, l. resting on parazonium at side.
410	AE 27.7 13.205	↓	Dp	IMP CAES VESPASIAN AVG COS IIII; head of Vespasian, radiate, r.	CONCO[R]DIA AVGVSTI; S C in ex.; Concordia seated l., holding patera in extending r. hand, in l., cornucopia.
411	AE 25.6 9.430	↓	As	IMP CAES VESPASIAN AVG [P P COS IIII]; head of Vespasian, laureate, r.	[AE]Q[VI]TAS AVG[VSTI]; S – C to l. and r. of Aequitas, standing l., holding scales in r. hand, in l. rod.
412	AE 27.0 17.710	↓	Dp	IMP CAES VESP AVG P M T P COS IIII CENS; head of Vespasian, radiate, l.	FELICITAS PVBLICA; S – C to l. and r. Felicitas, standing l., holding caduceus in r. hand, in l., cornucopiae.
413	AE 27.1 13.450	↓	Dp	Similar, but IMP CAES VESP AVG P M T P COS V CENS.	Similar.
414	AE 27.1 13.700	↓	Dp	IMP CAES VESP AVG P M T P COS VI; head of Vespasian, radiate, r.	Similar.

Of coins issued by the mint of Lugdunum

No.	Metal Size Weight	Axis	Denomination	Obverse	Reverse
415	AE 27.1 10.150	↓	Dp	[IMP CAES] VESPASIAN AVG COS VIII P P; head of Vespasian, laureate, r.	[F]IDES [P]VBLICA; S – C to l. and r.; Fides standing l., holding patera in r. hand, in l., cornucopiae.
416	AE 25.5 9.300	↓	Dp	Similar, but [IMP] CAES VESPASIAN AVG COS [VIII PP].	Similar, but FIDE[S PVBLICA].

TITUS

No.	Metal Size Weight	Axis	Denomination	Obverse	Reverse
417	AE 28.1 13.910	↓	Dp	T CAES IMP PON TR P COS II CENS; head of Titus, radiate, r.	FELICITAS PVBLICA, S – C to l. and r. Felicitas standing l., holding caduceus in r. hand, in l., cornucopiae.
418	AE 24.4 8.480	↓	As	[T CAES] VESPASIAN IMP P TR P COS II; head of Titus, laureate, r.	AEQVITAS AVGVSTI; S – C to l. and r. Aequitas, standing l., holding scales in r. hand, in l. rod.

No.	Metal Size Weight	Axis	Denomination	Obverse	Reverse

DOMITIAN

No.	Metal Size Weight	Axis	Denomination	Obverse	Reverse
419	AR 18.2 3.070	↓	D	CAESAR AVG F DOM-[ITIANVS], starting r.; head of Domitian, laureate, r.	[CE]RES [AV]GVST; Ceres, standing l., holding corn-ears in extending r. hand, in l. torch.

TITUS (A.D. 79–81)

Imperial Issues

Mint of Rome

A.D. 79 (June 23 – July 1)

No.	Metal Size Weight	Axis	Denomination	Obverse	Reverse
420	AR 19.2 2.600	↓	D	IMP T CAESAR VESPA-SIANVS AVG, starting r.; head of Titus, laureate, r.	TR POT VIII COS VII; male captive kneeling r., hands bound behind back, in front of trophy.

A.D. 79 (after July 1)

No.	Metal Size Weight	Axis	Denomination	Obverse	Reverse
421	AR 18.5 3.150	↓	D	IMP TITVS CAES VES-PASIAN AVG [P M], starting r.; head of Titus, laureate, r.	TR P VIIII IMP XIIII COS VII P P; Ceres seated l., holdind corn-ears in extended r. hand, in l., torch.
422	AR 18.7 3.010	↓	D	Similar, but [IMP] TITVS CAES VESPA[SIAN AVG P M].	TR P [VIIII IMP XIIII] COS VII P P; Venus, naked except for drapery round hip, standing r., leaning on cippus, holding helmet in extended r. hand, in l., spear.
423	AR 18.0 2.510	↓	D	Similar, but IMP TITVS CAES VESPASIAN AVG P M.	Similar, but TR P VIIII [IMP] XIIII COS VII P P.
424	AR 18.7 2.760	↓	D	Similar, but IMP TITVS VESP[ASIAN] AVG P M; head of Titus l.	TR P VIIII IMP XIIII COS VII [P P]; quadriga l., with corn-ears in ear.

---

[420] RIC 1, BMC 1.
[421] RIC 8, BMC 7.
[422] RIC 9, BMC 9.
[423] RIC 9, BMC 9.
[424] RIC 12, BMC 18.

No.	Metal Size Weight	Axis	Deno-mina-tion	Obverse	Reverse
425	AR 19.2 2.570	↓	D	Similar, but IMP TITVS VESPASIAN AVG P M; head of Titus r.	[TR P] VIIII [IMP XV] COS V[II P P]; capricorn l.; below, globe.
A.D. 80 (1 January – 1 July)					
426	AR 17.7 3.150	↓	D	IMP TITVS CAES VESPASIAN AVG P M, starting r.; head of Titus, laureate, r.	TR P IX IMP XV COS VIII P P; elephant, l.
427	AR 18.2 2.600	↓	D	Similar, but [IMP] TITVS CAES VESPASIAN AVG P M.	TR P IX IMP X[V] COS VIII P P; throne with round back, on which are corn-ears.
DOMITIAN (striking under Titus)					
A.D. 80					
428	AR 18.2 3.030	↓	D	[C]AESAR AVG F DOMITIANVS COS V[II], starting r.; head of Domitian, laureate, r.	PRINCEPS IVVENTVTIS; clasped hands, holding eagle on prow.
429	AR 17.6 3.150	↓	D	Similar, but CAESAR AVG F DOM[ITIANVS] COS VI[I].	Similar, but PRIN[CEPS] IVVENTVTIS.
A.D. 80 (later)					
430	AR 17.2 2.410	↓	D	CAESAR DIVI F DOMITIANVS COS VII, starting r.; head of Domitian, laureate, r.	PRINCE[PS] IVVENTVTIS: goat standing l. in laurel-wreath.
431	AR 18.3 2.970	↓	D	Similar.	PRINCEPS IVVE[NTVTIS]; altar, garlanded and lighted.
432	AR 18.0 2.750	↓	D	Similar.	Similar.

425 RIC 19, BMC 35.
426 RIC 22a, BMC 43.
427 RIC 24a, BMC 14.
428 RIC 45, BMC 85.
429 RIC 45, BMC 85.
430 RIC 49, BMC 88.
431 RIC 50, BMC 92.
432 RIC 50, BMC 92.

No.	Metal Size Weight	Axis	Denomination	Obverse	Reverse
433	AR 18.8 2.790	↓	D	Similar.	PRINCEPS IVVENTVTIS; helmet on throne.
434	AR 18.0 3.030	↓	D	Similar, but [CAESAR DIVI F DOMI]TIANVS COS VII.	Similar, but [PRIN]CEPS IVVENTV[TIS].

DIVVS VESPASIANVS

A.D. 80 – 81

No.	Metal Size Weight	Axis	Denomination	Obverse	Reverse
435	AR 19.2 3.235	↓	D	DIVVS AVGVSTVS VESPASIANVS; head of Vespasian, laureate, r.	[S C] on shield, supported by two capricorns; below, globe.

AES

Mint of Rome
A.D. 80

No.	Metal Size Weight	Axis	Denomination	Obverse	Reverse
436	AE 27.3 10.330	↓	Dp	IMP T CAES VESP AVG P M TR P COS VIII; head of Titus, radiate, l.	VESTA in ex.; S – C to l. and r.; Vesta, veiled seated l., holding palladium in extended r. hand, in l., sceptre.
437	AE 28.2 11.430	↓	Dp	Similar, but IMP T VESP [AVG P] M [TR P] COS VIII.	Similar, but VES[TA].
438	AE 28.8 9.400	↓	As	Similar, but IMP T CAE S VESP AVG P M TR P COS VII I; head of Titus l.	AEQVI [TAS] AVGVSTI; S – C to l. and r. Aequitas standing l., holding scales in r. hand, in l., rod.

433 RIC 51, BMC 98.
434 RIC 51, BMC 98.
435 RIC 63, BMC 132.
436 RIC 120b, BMC 201.
437 RIC 120b, BMC 201.
438 RIC 121b, BMC 205.

No.	Metal Size Weight	Axis	Denomination	Obverse	Reverse

DIOMITIAN (striking under Titus)

A.D. 80–81

No.	Metal Size Weight	Axis	Denomination	Obverse	Reverse
439	AE 28.3 12.330	↓	Dp	CAES DIVI VESP F DOMITIAN COS VII; head of Domitian, laureate, l.	S –C to l. and r.; Minerva standing l., holding thunderbolt in r. hand, in l., spear; at her feet, shield.
440	AE 28.2 10.550	↓	As	Similar.	Similar.

Mint of Lugdunum
A.D. 80–81

No.	Metal Size Weight	Axis	Denomination	Obverse	Reverse
441	AE 28.0 11.710	↓	Dp	IMP T CAES DIVI VESP F [A]VG P M TR [P P P] COS VIII; head of Titus, radiate, r.	ROMA; S C in ex. Roma in military dress seated l. on cuirass, holding wreath in extended r. hand, in l. parazonium.

Forgeries

Of coins issued by the mint of Rome

No.	Metal Size Weight	Axis	Denomination	Obverse	Reverse
442	AE 32.7 23.100	↓	S	IMP T CAES VESP AVG P M TR P P P COS VIII; head of Titus, laureate, l.	PROVIDENT AVGVST; SC in ex.; Vespasian, radiate, standing l., presenting a globe to Titus, who stands r.; between them, rudder (?).
443	AE 35.2 27.980	↑	S	IMP T CAES VESP AVG P M TR P P P COS VIII; head of Titus, laureate, l.	S –C to l. and r.; Mars advancing r., holding transverse spear in r. hand and trophy over l. shoulder.
444	AE 24.9 8.900	↓	As	IMP T CAES VESP [AVG P M TR P] COS VIII; head of Titus, laureate, r.	AEQVITAS AVGVSTI; S – C to l. and r.; Aequitas standing l., holding scales in r. hand, in l., rod.

---

439 RIC 169b, BMC 246.
440 RIC 169b, BMC 246.
441 RIC 183.

No.	Metal Size Weight	Axis	Denomination	Obverse	Reverse
DOMITIAN					
445	AR 17.2 3.015	↓	D	CAESAR DIVI F DOMITIANVS COS VII, starting r.; head of Domitian, laureate, r.	PRINCEPS [IV]VENTVTIS; goat standing l. in laurel-wreath.

DOMITIAN (A.D. 81–96)

Imperial Issues

Mint of Rome
A.D. 81 – First Issue

No.	Metal Size Weight	Axis	Denomination	Obverse	Reverse
446	AR 18.1 3.210	↓	D	IMP CAESAR DOMITIANVS AVG, starting r.; head of Domitian, laureate, r.	TR P COS VII; throne, decked with corn-ears.
447	AR 19.2 2.510	↓	D	Similar.	TR P COS VII; tripod on which are: ravens and dolphin.
Third Issue					
448	AR 19.2 3.200	↓	D	IMP CAES DOMITIANVS AVG P M, starting r.; head of Domitian, laureate, r.	TR P COS VII [DE]S VIII P P; thunderbolt on throne.
449	AR 18.7 3.060	↓	D	IMP CAES DOMITIANVS AVG P M, starting r.; head of Domitian, laureate, r.	TR P [CO]S VII DES VIII P P; Minerva standing l., holding Victory in extended r. hand, in l. spear: at feet, shield.
A.D. 82 – First Issue					
450	AR 18.5 3.020	↓	D	IMP CAES DOMITIANVS AVG P M, starting r.; head of Domitian, laureate, r.	TR POT COS VIII P P; dolphin twined round anchor.

---

[446] RIC 2, BMC 2.
[447] RIC 3, BMC 4.
[448] RIC 16, BMC 16.
[449] RIC 23, BMC 13.
[450] RIC 28, BMC 29.

No.	Metal Size Weight	Axis	Denomination	Obverse	Reverse
A.D. 88–89 Fourth Issue					
451	AR 19.6 3.210	↓	D	IMP CAES DOMIT AVG [GE]RM P M TR P VIII; head of Domitian, laureate, r.	IMP XIX COS XIIII CENS P P P; Minerva advancing r., brandishing javelin in r. hand and holding shield on l.
452	AR 18.6 3.270	↓	D	Similar, but IMP CAES DOMIT AVG GERM P M TR P VIII.	IMP XIX COS XIIII CENS P P P; Minerva standing l., holding thunderbolt in r. hand, in l. spear; at feet, shield.
Fifth Issue					
453	AR 18.9 2.940	↓	D	IMP CAES DOMIT AVG GERM P M TR P V[III]; head of Domitian, laureate, r.	IMP [XXI] COS XIIII CENS P P P; Minerva advancing r., brandishing javelin in r. hand and holding shield in l.
A.D. 89					
454	AR 19.6 2.640	↓	D	IMP CAES DOMIT AVG GERM [P M TR P] VIIII; head of Domitian, laureate, r.	[IMP XXI COS] XIIII [CENS P P P]; Minerva standing l., holding spear in r. hand.
A.D. 90					
455	AR 19.1 2.190	↓	D	IMP CAES DOMIT AVG GERM P M TR P [V]IIII; head of Domitian, laureate r.	IMP XXI COS XV CENS P P P; Minerva advancing r., brandishing javelin in r. hand and holding shield on l.
456	AR 18.8 3.145	↓	D	Similar, but [IMP] CAES DOMIT AVG GERM P M TR P [VIIII].	Similar.
457	AR 18.8 3.150	↓	D	Similar, but [IMP] CAES DOMIT AVG GERM P M TR P VIIII.	IMP XXI COS XV CENS P P P; Minerva standing l., holding thunderbolt in r. hand, in l. spear; at feet, shield.

---

[451] RIC 137, BMC 147.
[452] RIC 139, BMC 153.
[453] RIC 142, BMC 158.
[454] RIC 146, BMC 163.
[455] RIC 147, BMC 164.
[456] RIC 147, BMC 164.
[457] RIC 149, BMC 167.

No.	Metal Size Weight	Axis	Denomination	Obverse	Reverse
458	AR 18.6 3.200	↓	D	Similar, but IMP CAES DOMIT AVG GERM P M TR P VIIII.	IMP XXI CO[S] XV CENS P P P; Minerva standing l., holding spear in r. hand.
A.D. 91					
459	AR 18.4 2.920	↓	D	[IMP CAE]S DOMIT AVG GERM P M TR P XI; head of Domitian, laureate, r.	IMP XXI COS XV CENS P P P; Minerva standing l., holding spear in r. hand.
A.D. 92					
460	AR 17.5 2.985	↓	D	[IMP C]AES DOMIT AVG GERM P M TR P XI; head of Domitian, laureate, r.	[IMP] XXI COS XVI CENS P P P; Minerva standing l., holding spear in r. hand.
A.D. 92–93					
461	AR 19.2 3.200	↙		IMP CAES DOMIT AVG GERM P M TR P XII; head of Domitian, laureate, r.	IMP XXII COS XVI CENS P P P; Minerva advancing r., brandishing javelin in r. hand and holding shield on l.
462	AR 18.7 3.400	↓	D	Similar, but [IMP CA]ES DOMIT AVG GERM P M TR P XII.	IMP XXII CO[S XVI CEN]S P P P; Minerva standing l., holding thunderbolt in r. hand, in l. spear; at feet, shield.
A.D. 93–94					
463	AR 18.2 3.265	↓	D	[IMP] CAES DOMIT AVG GERM P M TR P XIII; head of Domitian, laureate, r.	IMP XXII COS XVI CENS P P P; Minerva standing r. on prow, brandishing javelin in r. hand and holding shield on l.; at feet, r., owl.
A.D. 94					
464	AR 19.7 3.050	↓	D	[I]MP CAES DOMIT AVG GERM P M TR P XIIII; head of Domitian, laureate, r.	IMP XXII[COS] XVIICENS P P P; Minerva standing r. on prow, brandishing javelin in r. hand and holding shield on l.; at feet, r., owl.

[458] RIC 150, BMC 168.
[459] RIC 159, BMC 186.
[460] RIC 169, BMC 194.
[461] RIC 171, BMC 200.
[462] RIC 173, BMC 205.
[463] RIC 174, BMC 216.
[464] RIC 179, BMC p. 341, +.

No.	Metal Size Weight	Axis	Denomination	Obverse	Reverse
A.D. 95–96					
465	AR 19.3 3.310	↙	D	IMP CAES DOMIT AVG GERM P M TR P XV; head of Domitian, laureate, r.	IMP XXII COS XVII CENS P P P; Minerva advancing r., brandishing javelin in r. hand and holding shield on l.
466	AR 18.3 3.130	↓	D	Similar.	IMP XXII COS XVII CENS P P P; Minerva standing l., holding thunderbolt in r. hand and spear in l.; at feet, shield.

AES

Mint of Rome
A.D. 82

No.	Metal Size Weight	Axis	Denomination	Obverse	Reverse
467	AE 32.5 22.160	↓	S	[IMP CAE]S DIVI VESP F DOMITIAN AVG P M; head of Domitian, laureate, r.	TR P CO[S VIII DE]S VIIII P P; S – C to l. and P; Minerva advancing r., brandishing javelin in r. hand and holding shield on l.
468	AE 24.7 11.050	↓	As	Similar, but [IMP CAES] DIVI VESP F DOMITIAN AVG [P M].	Similar, but [TR P COS VIII] DES VIIII P P.
A.D. 85					
469	AE 29.3 11.500	↓	Dp	[IMP] CAES DOMITIAN AVG GER[M COS XI]; bust of Domitian, radiate, r., with aegis.	FORTVNAE [A]VGVSTI; S – C to l. and r.; Fortuna standing l., holding rudder in r. hand and cornucopiae in l.
470	AE 27.8 10.680	↓	As	IMP CAES D[OMI]T AVG GERM COS XI CENS POT P P; bust of Domitian, with aegis, r., head laureate.	S – C to l. and r.; Victory advancing l., holding in r. hand shield inscribed S P Q R; l. hand on side.

465 RIC 190, BMC 230.
466 RIC 192, BMC 234.
467 RIC 239a, BMC 272.
468 RIC 242a, BMC 281.
469 RIC –, BMC p. 365, +.
470 RIC 302a, BMC 355.

No.	Metal Size Weight	Axis	Denomination	Obverse	Reverse
A.D. 87					
471	AE 29.8 10.770	↓	As	IMP CAES DOMIT AVG GERM COS XIII CENS P[ER]P P; bust of Domitian, head laureate, r.	FIDEI PVBLICAE; S–C to l. and r.; Fides standing r., holding corn-ears downwards in r. hand and basket of fruits in l.
472	AE 26.5 9.360	↓	As	Similar.	VIRTVTI AVGVSTI; S–C to l. and r.; Virtus standing r., l. foot set on helmet, holding spear in r. hand and parazonium in l.
473	AE 27.1 10.230	↓	As	Similar, but IMP CAES DOMIT AVG GERM COS XIII [CENS PER P P], with aegis.	Similar, but VIRT[VTI AVGVSTI].
A.D. 90–91					
474	AE 28.0 12.000	↓	Dp	IMP CAES DOMIT AVG GERM COS XV CENS PER [P P]; head of Domitian, radiate, r.	[F]ORTVN[AE A]VGVSTI; S – C to l. and r.; Fortune standing l., holding rudder in r. hand and cornucopiae in l.
475	AE 28.3 12.150	↓	Dp	Similar, but [IMP CAES DO]MIT AVG GERM COS X[V CE]NS [PER P P].	Similar, but FORTVN[AE AVGVSTI].
476	AE 30.5 10.850	↙	As	IMP CAES DOMIT AVG GERM COS XV CENS PER P P; head of Domitian, laureate, r.	Similar, but FORTVNAE AVGVSTI.
477	AE 27.2 11.810	↓	As	IMP CAES DOMIT AVG GE[RM COS XV CE]NS PER P P; head of Domitian, laureate, r.	MONETA A[VGVSTI]; S –C to l. and r. Moneta standing l., holding scales in r. hand and cornucopiae in l.

471 RIC 352, BMC 385.
472 RIC 356, BMC 393.
473 RIC 356b, BMC 393.
474 RIC 392, BMC 444.
475 RIC 392, BMC 444.
476 RIC 394, BMC 448.
477 RIC 395, BMC 449.

No.	Metal Size Weight	Axis	Denomination	Obverse	Reverse
478	AE 29.1 11.600	↘	As	IMP CAES DOMIT AVG GERM COS XV CENS PER [P P]; head of Domitian, laureate, r.	VIRTVTI AVGVSTI; S – C to l. and r.: Virtus standing r., l. foot set on helmet, holding spear in r. hand and parazonium in l.
A.D. 92–94					
479	AE 34.0 26.410	↓	As	IMP CAES DOMIT AVG GERM COS XVI CENS PER P P; head of Domitian, laureate, r.	IOVI VICTORI; SC in ex. Jupiter, naked to hips, seated l., holding Victory in extended r. hand and sceptre in l.
Undated					
480	AE 16.0 2.965	↙	Quad.	IMP DOMIT AV[G GE]-RM; in centre, S C.	Rhinoceros r.
481	AE 19.0 2.815	↗	Quad.	Similar, but IMP DOMIT AVG GERM.	Similar.
482	AE 16.8 2.000	↑	Quad.	Similar, but IMP [DO]-MIT AVG GERM.	Rhinoceros l.
483	AE 15.3 2.520	↓	Quad.	IMP DOM TI (!) AV[G]; bust of Minerva, helmeted, r.	S C in laurel-wreath.

Restorations

DIVVS AVGVSTVS

No.	Metal Size Weight	Axis	Denomination	Obverse	Reverse
484	AE 25.6 8.465	↓	As	DIVVS AVGVSTVS PA-[TER]; head of Divus Augustus, radiate, l.	IMP D CAES AVG [RESTI]-TVIT; S – C to l. and r. head of eagle; eagle standing to front on globe, head r.

---

478 RIC 397, BMC 452.
479 RIC 401, BMC 464.
480 RIC 434, BMC 496.
481 RIC 434, BMC 496.
482 RIC 435, BMC 498.
483 RIC 428, BMC 486 (?).
484 RIC 456, BMC 506.

No.	Metal Size Weight	Axis	Denomination	Obverse	Reverse
GERMANICVS					
485	AE 26.0 9.750	↓	As	GERMANICVS CAESAR TI [AVG] F DIVI AVG N; head of Germanicus, bare, l.	IMP D CAES DIVI VESP AVG REST; in centre, S C.
Mint of Antioch					
486	AE 24.7 10.070	↗	As	[IMP DOMITIANVS CAES AVG]; head of Domitian, laureate, l.	S C in laurel-wreath.

Forgeries

Of coins issued by the mint of Rome

No.	Metal Size Weight	Axis	Denomination	Obverse	Reverse
487	AR 18.4 3.370	↓	D	IMP CAES DOMITIANVS AVG P M, starting r.; head of Domitian, laureate, r.	COS VII DES VIII P P; thunderbolt on throne.
488	AE 27.2 11.475	↓	Dp	[IMP] CAES DIVI VESP F DOMITIAN AVG P M; head of Domitian, radiate, r.	TR P COS [VII DES VIII P P]; S – C to l. and r.; Minerva standing l., holding thunderbolt in r. hand and spear in l.
489	AE 33.5 22.420	↘	S	IMP CAES DIV VESP F DOMITIAN AVG P M; head of Domitian, laureate, l.	TR P COS VIII DES VIIII P P; S – C to l. and r.; Minerva standing l., holding spear in r. hand.
490	AE 27.2 12.900	↓	As	Similar, but head of Domitian r.	TR P COS VIII [DES VIIII P P]; Minerva advancing r., brandishing javelin in r. hand and holding shield on l.
491	AE 30.0 11.240	↙	As	IMP CAES DOMIT AVG GERM COS XII PER P P; bust of Domitian with aegis, r.; head laureate.	FORTVNAE AVGVSTI; S – C to l. and r.; Fortuna standing l., holding rudder in r. hand and cornucopiae in l.
492	AE 26.5 9.420	↓	As	No legend; bust of Domitian with aegis, r., head laureate.	SAL[VTI] AVGVSTI; S–C to l. and r. of altar.

---

485 RIC 460, BMC 511.

486 BMC Galatia, Cappadotia, Syria 245.

No.	Metal Size Weight	Axis	Deno- mina- tion	Obverse	Reverse
493	AE 25.6 9.580	↓	As	IMP CAES DOMIT AVG GER COS XIII CENS; head of Domitian, laureate, r.	COS VIII DES VIIII; S –C to l. and r.; Minerva advancing r., brandishing javelin in r. hand and holding shield on l.

Index of emperors and their relatives

Kings

Index of types

Index of legends

Numerals

Index of moneyers

Index of Greek legends

Numerals

Index of mints

Concordance

Number of the Catalogue	Inventory number
1	796
2	795
3	792
4	849
5	848
6	4113
7	815
8	829
9	860
10	789
11	791
12	793
13	4111
14	4110
15	3992
16	3993
17	3968
18	3994
19	3973
20	3974
21	3987
22	3975
23	3988
24	4032
25	3995
26	4283
27	3951
28	811
29	3967
30	812
31	813
32	4031
33	4030
34	3990
35	3989
36	4114
37	814
38	830
39	831
40	794
41	799
42	817
43	4197
44	4189
45	4190
46	4191

Number of the Catalogue	Inventory number
47	5815
48	4301
49	4302
50	4481
51	5818
52	4454
53	4482
54	4453
55	4391
56	122
57	123
58	786
59	4366
60	4214
61	816
62	4246
63	5820
64	4057
65	790
66	4443
67	788
68	5577
69	4125
70	5813
71	800
72	846
73	4130
74	853
75	854
76	856
77	857
78	858
79	859
80	884
81	4090
82	843
83	845
84	3953
85	887
86	850
87	851
88	4055
89	852
90	805
91	806
92	807

Number of the Catalogue	Inventory number
93	808
94	818
95	819
96	820
97	821
98	822
99	823
100	824
101	825
102	826
103	828
104	3950
105	803
106	804
107	3970
108	802
109	4369
110	4335
111	4485
112	5817
113	4486
114	847
115	4117
116	844
117	855
118	4123
119	827
120	4000
121	801
122	4194
123	872
124	882
125	861
126	862
127	870
128	868
129	869
130	864
131	933
132	934
133	886
134	885
135	865
136	832
137	834
138	835

Number of the Catalogue	Inventory number	Number of the Catalogue	Inventory number	Number of the Catalogue	Inventory number
139	836	190	874	241	374
140	837	191	875	242	4142
141	838	192	5345	243	369
142	840	193	4392	244	370
143	841	194	4483	245	785
144	4112	195	4484	246	784
145	4387	196	4325	247	367
146	809	197	4326	248	368
147	4186	198	4327	249	375
148	4185	199	4328	250	4143
149	871	200	4329	251	371
150	889	201	4330	252	372
151	954	202	4331	253	373
152	932	203	4332	254	4281
153	863	204	4333	255	4389
154	883	205	4334	256	4336
155	866	206	4282	257	4337
156	4354	207	928	258	4339
157	839	208	891	259	4340
158	833	209	3976	260	4341
159	943	210	939	261	4390
160	945	211	877	262	4388
161	3991	212	926	263	4338
162	946	213	3871	264	4342
163	947	214	924	265	4280
164	867	215	925	266	4487
165	888	216	918	267	4488
166	944	217	931	268	931
167	927	218	896	269	893
168	935	219	899	270	895
169	880	220	4054	271	902
170	937	221	900	272	922
171	810	222	908	273	903
172	955	223	909	274	905
173	890	224	910	275	906
174	936	225	911	276	897
175	878	226	913	277	930
176	938	227	4087	278	912
177	940	228	4058	279	920
178	876	229	907	280	5801
179	948	230	898	281	4431
180	949	231	901	282	961
181	950	232	894	283	962
182	4091	233	919	284	963
183	881	234	904	285	964
184	879	235	917	286	965
185	929	236	915	287	4376
186	942	237	916	288	966
187	941	238	951	289	967
188	873	239	923	290	957
189	4140	240	4310	291	958

Number of the Catalogue	Inventory number	Number of the Catalogue	Inventory number	Number of the Catalogue	Inventory number
292	4313	343	992	394	1096
293	376	344	990	395	503
294	956	345	1020	396	977
295	960	346	1019	397	1009
296	958	347	1035	398	1055
297	969	348	1046	399	1831
298	968	349	1021	400	1056
299	3971	350	3872	401	1048
300	971	351	987	402	1053
301	972	352	1032	403	1060
302	4080	353	1518	404	4009
303	4079	354	3878	405	1052
304	970	355	1069	406	1050
305	973	356	1071	407	1012
306	976	357	1072	408	1830
307	975	358	1075	409	1049
308	1519	359	1074	410	4007
309	1829	360	1073	411	3943
310	993	361	1010	412	996
311	994	362	1011	413	1001
312	995	363	1013	414	999
313	1023	364	1014	415	1007
314	980	365	1015	416	3877
315	981	366	1039	417	1058
316	983	367	1047	418	979
317	984	368	1038	419	4029
318	4039	369	997	420	1068
319	4038	370	1834	421	1065
320	1037	371	1044	422	1062
321	982	372	1054	423	1061
322	985	373	1008	424	1064
323	986	374	1041	425	1066
324	1045	375	1042	426	1063
325	1833	376	1040	427	1067
326	1031	377	978	428	1105
327	1832	378	998	429	1106
328	1033	379	3944	430	1098
329	4077	380	3945	431	1101
330	1034	381	1000	432	1100
331	1024	382	1016	433	1102
332	1025	383	1006	434	1103
333	1026	384	1017	435	1051
334	1027	385	4148	436	1530
335	1028	386	1005	436	1530
336	4076	387	1022	437	1528
337	988	388	1002	438	4124
338	989	389	1003	439	1104
339	1029	390	1004	440	1107
340	1030	391	1018	441	1529
341	1036	392	3879	442	3884
342	991	393	1059	443	4120

Number of the Catalogue	Inventory number	Number of the Catalogue	Inventory number	Number of the Catalogue	Inventory number
444	1057	461	1083	478	1120
445	1097	462	1086	479	1095
446	1110	463	1087	480	1123
447	1109	464	1093	481	1122
448	1111	465	1092	482	1124
449	1112	466	1094	483	1125
450	1113	467	1116	484	4057
451	1079	468	1117	485	3952
452	1076	469	3876	486	4193
453	1078	470	1108	487	1088
454	1084	471	1089	488	1531
455	1080	472	1119	489	1115
456	4078	473	1121	490	1118
457	1077	474	1114	491	1090
458	1082	475	4016	492	4317
459	1081	476	1091	493	3946
460	1085	477	1099		

Plates

1
2
3
4
5
6
7
8
9
10
11
12

13
14
15
16
17
18
19
20
21
22
23
24

25
26
27
28
29
30
31
32
33
34
35
36
37

38
39
40
41
42
43
44
45
46
47
48

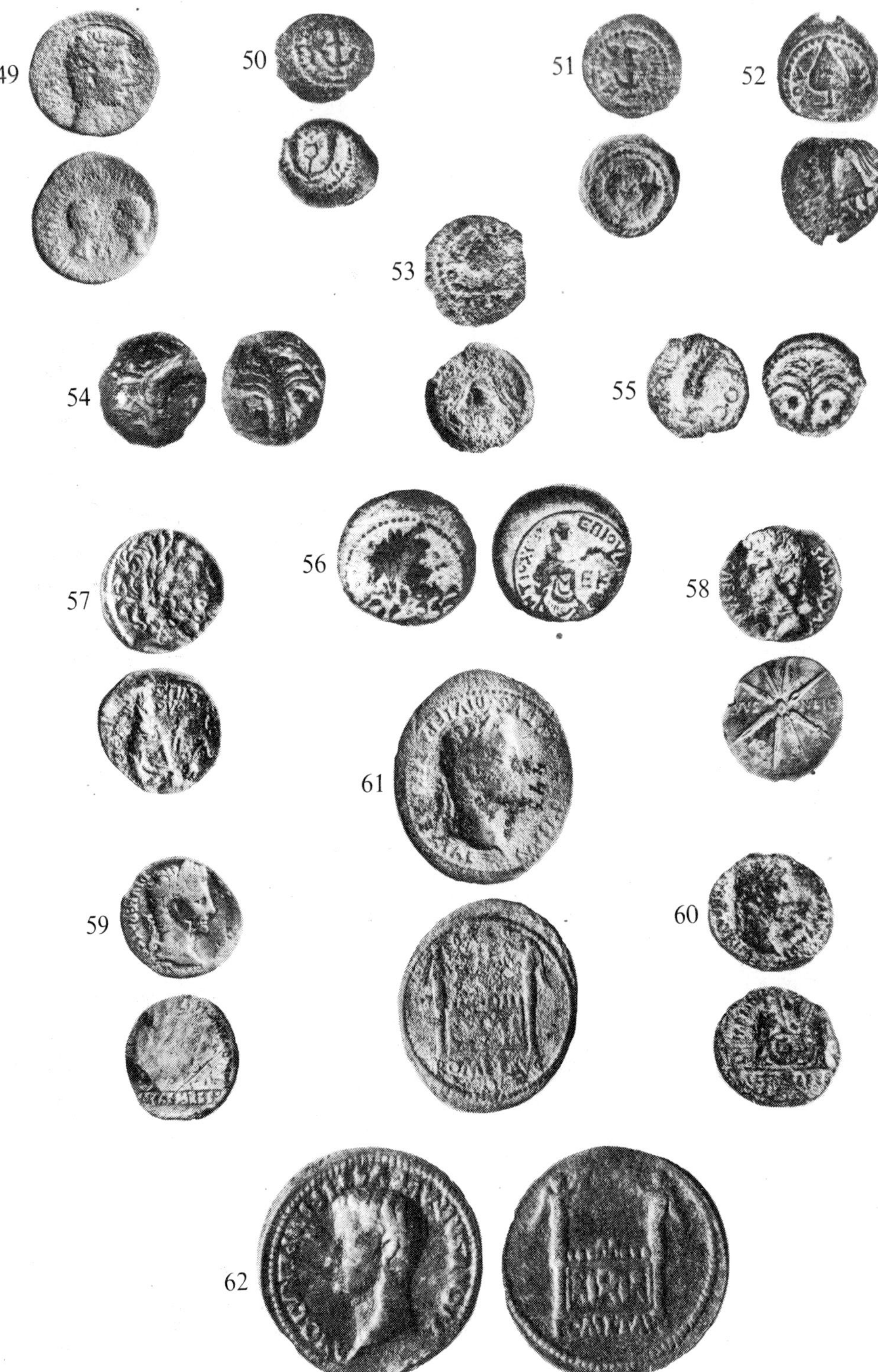
49
50
51
52
53
54
55
56
57
58
61
59
60
62

63
64
65
66
67
68
69
70
SC
71
SC
72

73
74
75
76
77
78
79
80
81

82
83
84
85
86
87
88
89
90

91
92
93
94
95
96
97
98
99

100
101
102
103
104
105
106
107
108
PROVIDENT
AVGVSTVS

109 

110

111

112

113

114

115

116

117

118

119
120
121
122
123
124
125
126
127

128
129
130
131
132
133
134
135
136
137

138
139
140
141
142
143
144
145
146

147
148
149
150
151
152
153
154
155

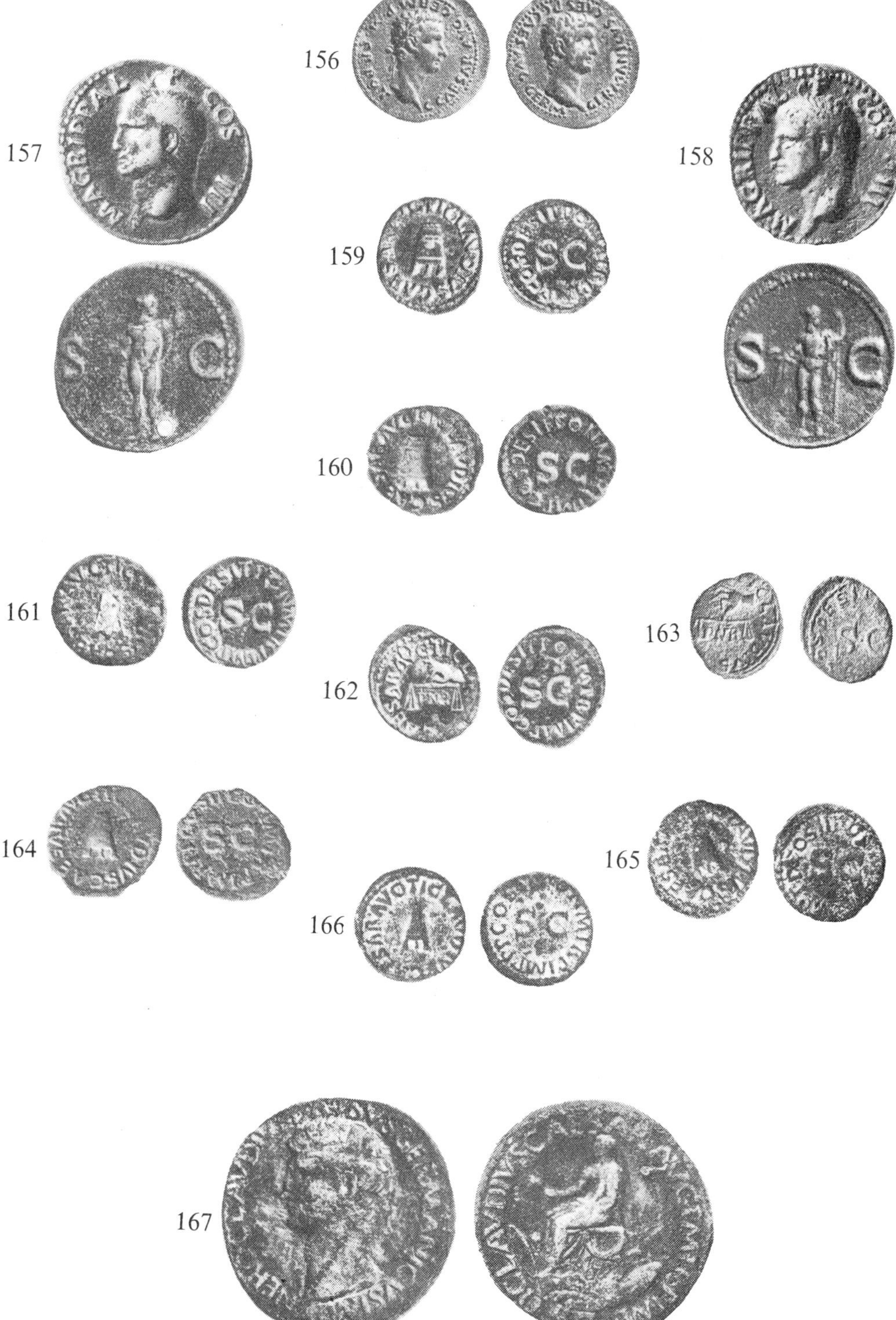
156
157
158
159
160
161
162
163
164
165
166
167

168
169
170
171
172
173
174
175

176
177
178
179
180
181
182
183

184
185
186
187
188
189
190
191
192

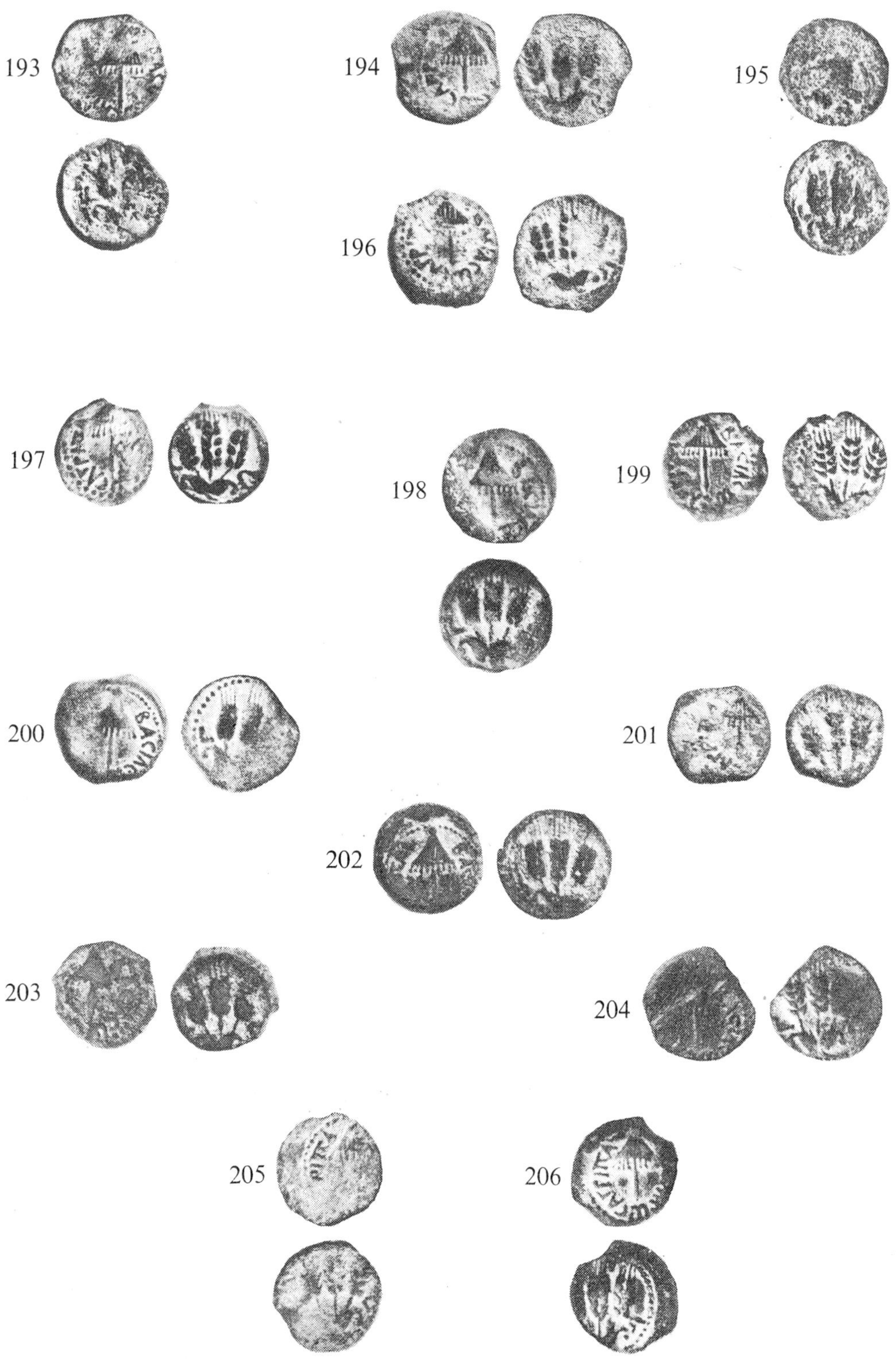
193
194
195
196
197
198
199
200
201
202
203
204
205
206

207
208
209
210
211
212
213
214
215

216
217
218
219
220
221
222
223
224

225
226
227
228
229
230
231
232

233
234
235
236
237
238
239
240
241

242
243
244
245
246
247
248
249
250
251
252
253

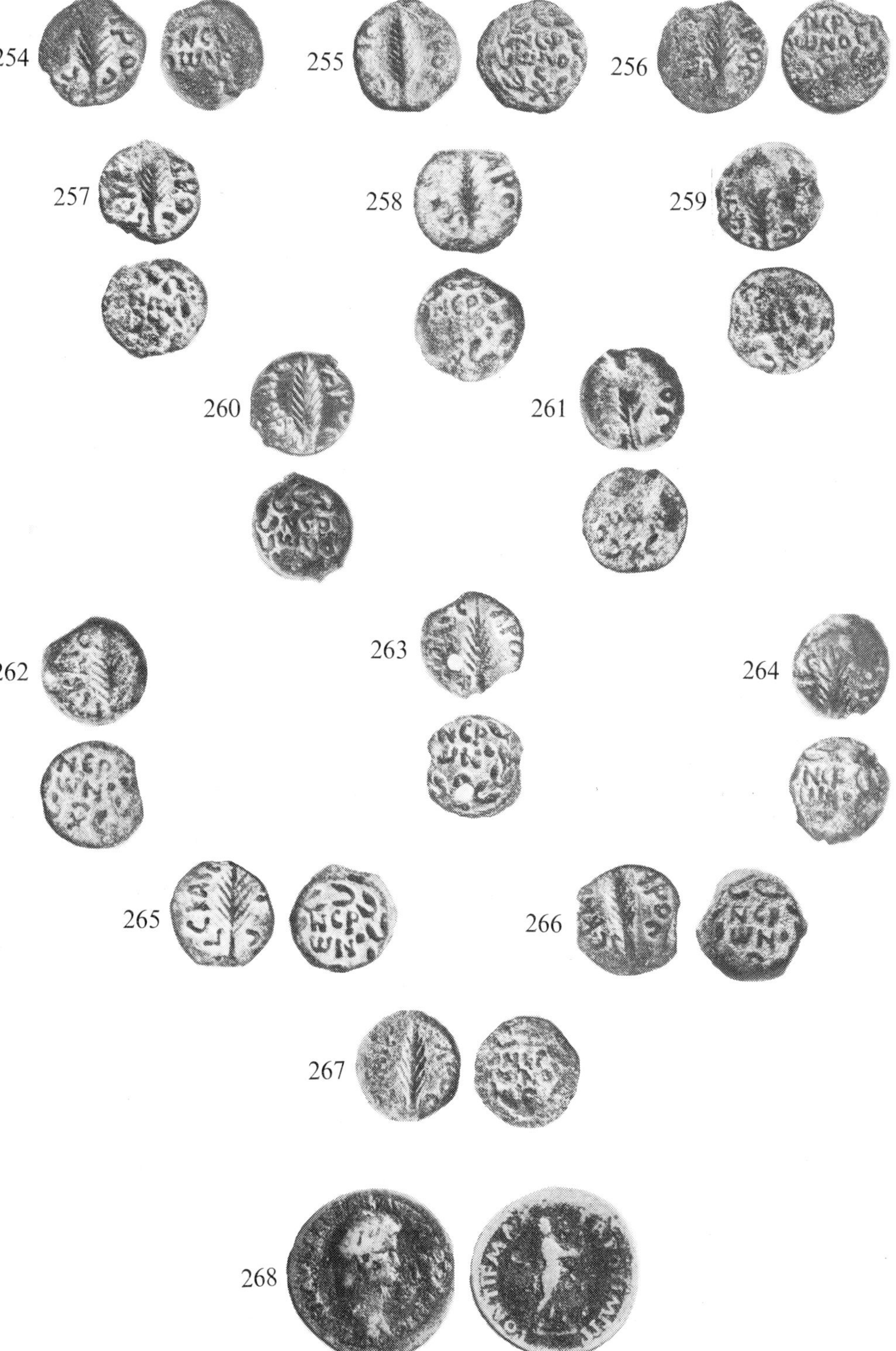
254
255
256
257
258
259
260
261
262
263
264
265
266
267
268

269
270
271
272
273
274
275

276
277
278
279
280
281
282
283
284
285
286

287
288
289
290
291
292
293
294

295
297
296
S POR
OB
CIVSER
298
299
300
303
301
302
S POR
OB
304
305
306

307
308
309
310
311
312
313
314
315
316
317
318
319
320
322
321
323

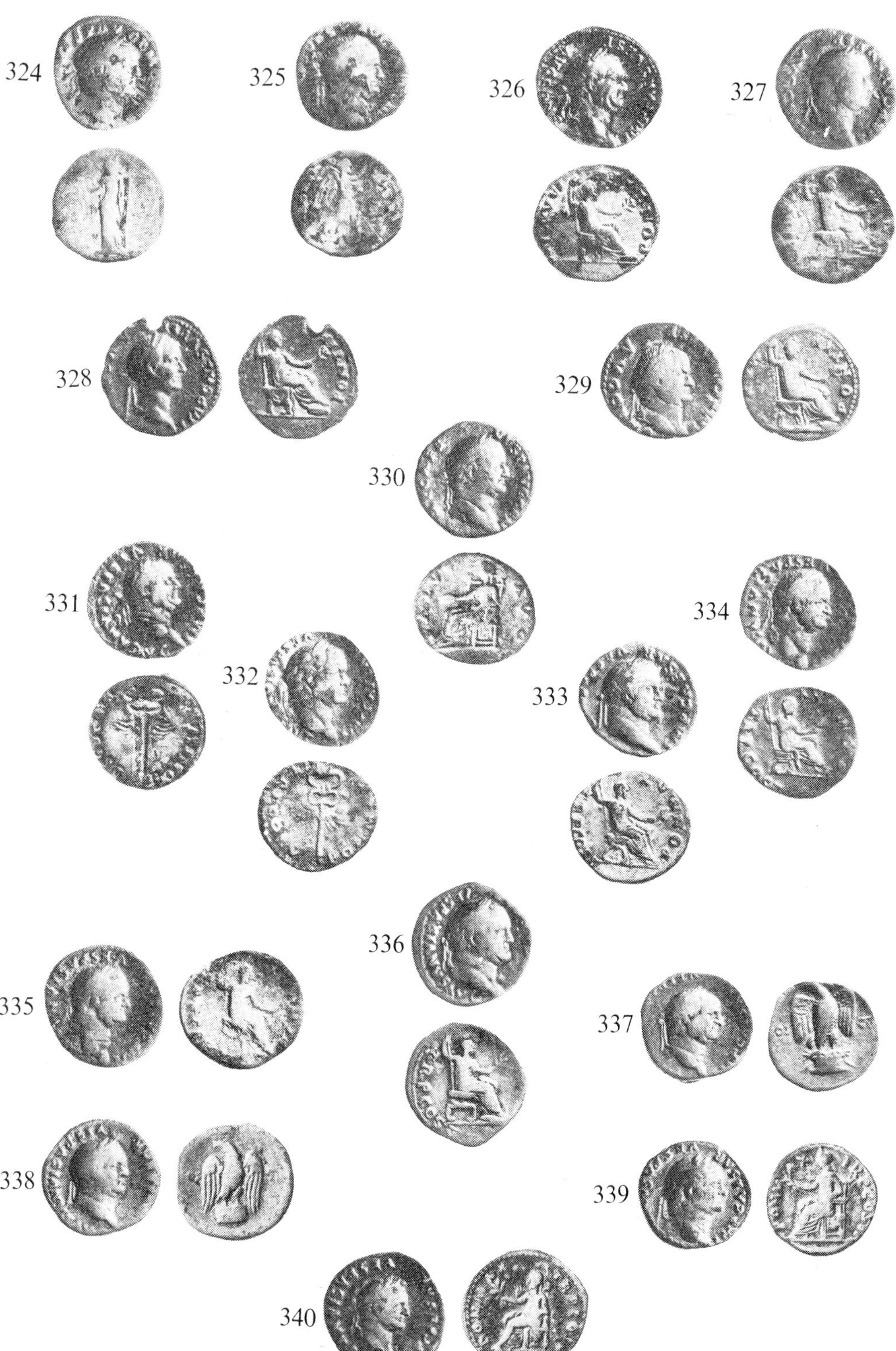
324
325
326
327
328
329
330
331
332
333
334
335
336
337
338
339
340

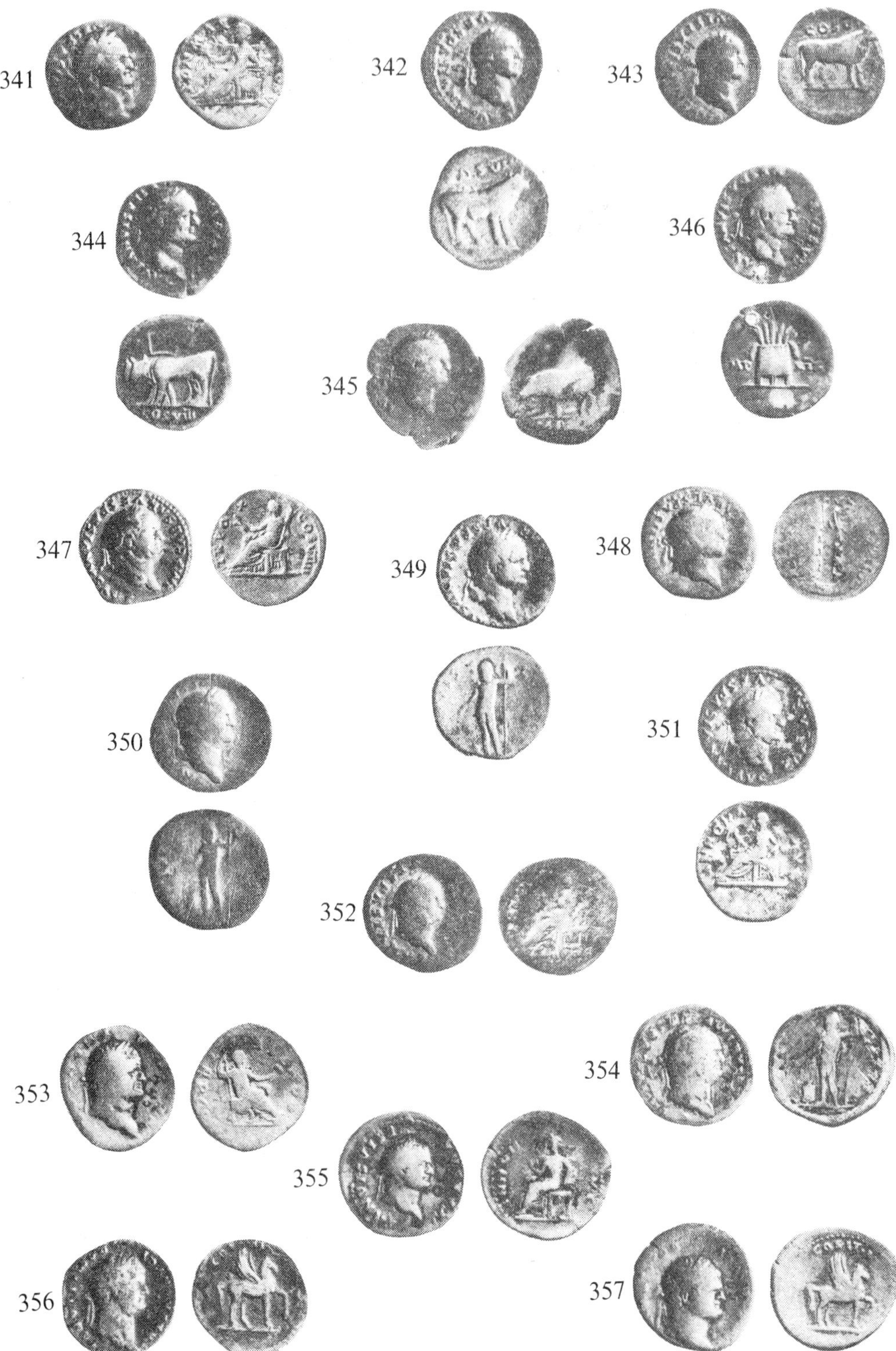
341
342
343
344
345
346
347
349
348
350
351
352
353
354
355
356
357

358
359
360
361
362
363
364
365
366

367
368
369
370
371
372
373
374
375

376
377
378
379
380
381
382
383
384

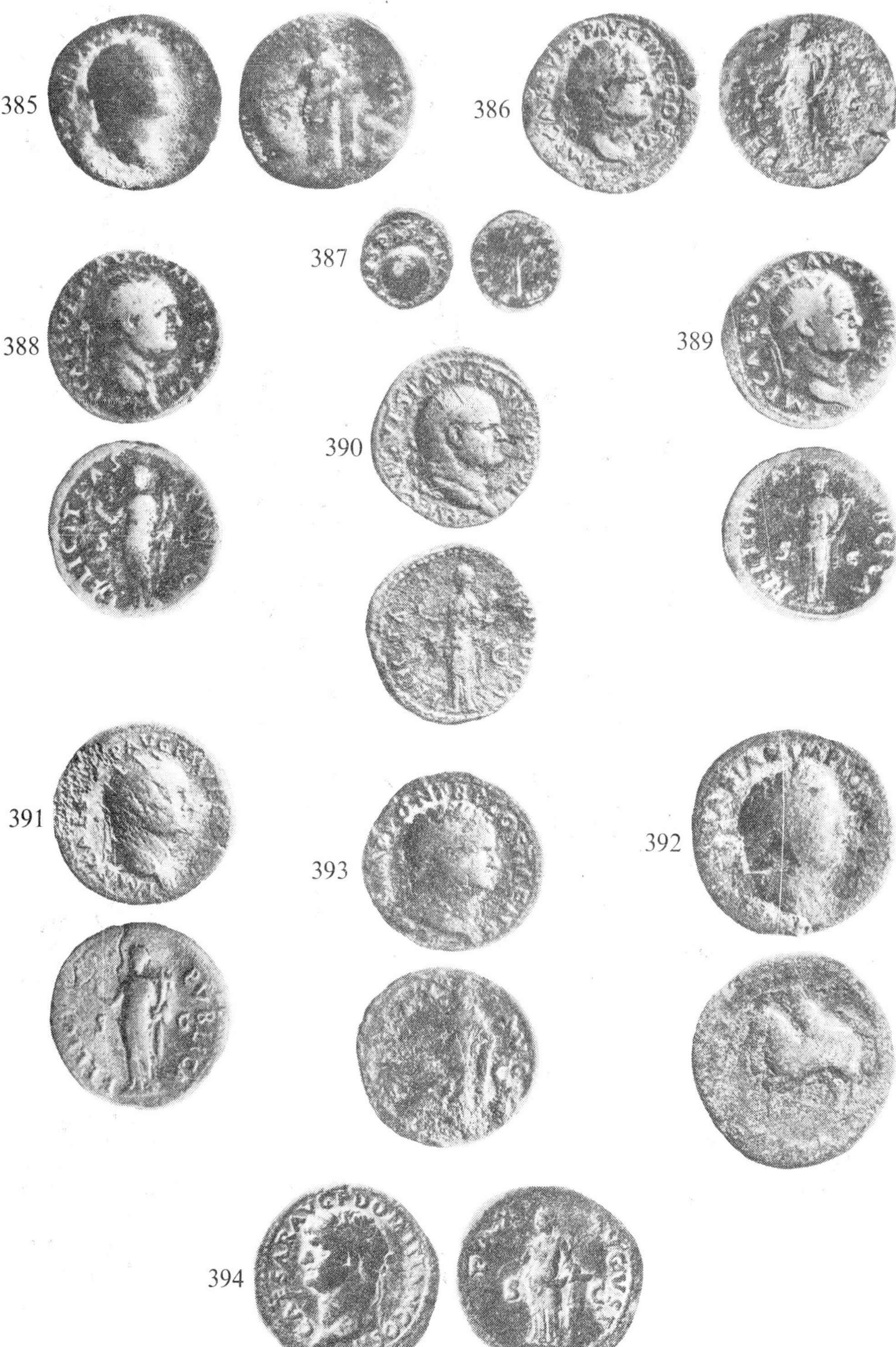
385
386
387
388
389
390
391
393
392
394

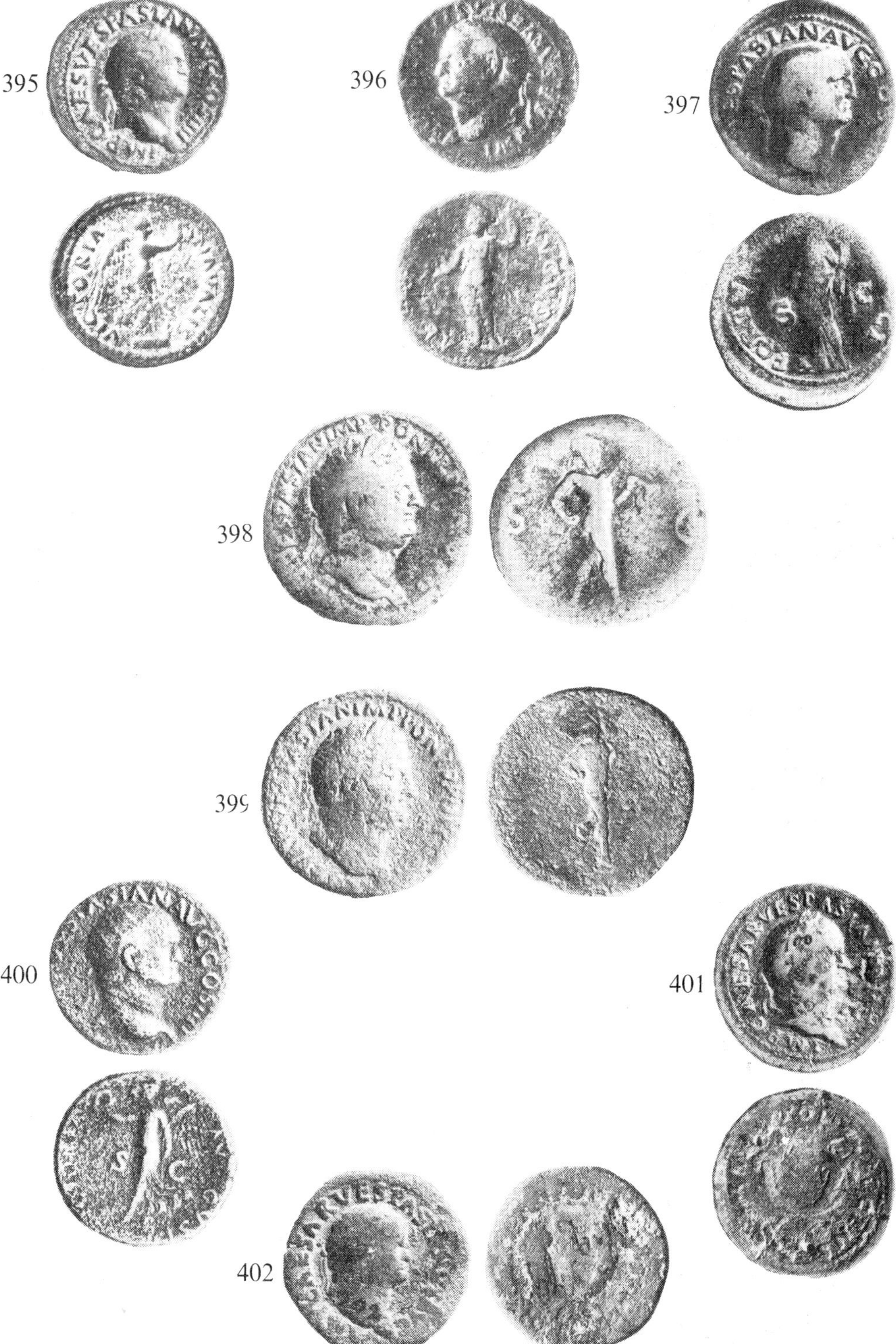
395
396
397
398
399
400
401
402

403
404
405
406
407
408
409
410
411
ROMA

412
413
414
415
416
417
418
419
420
421
422

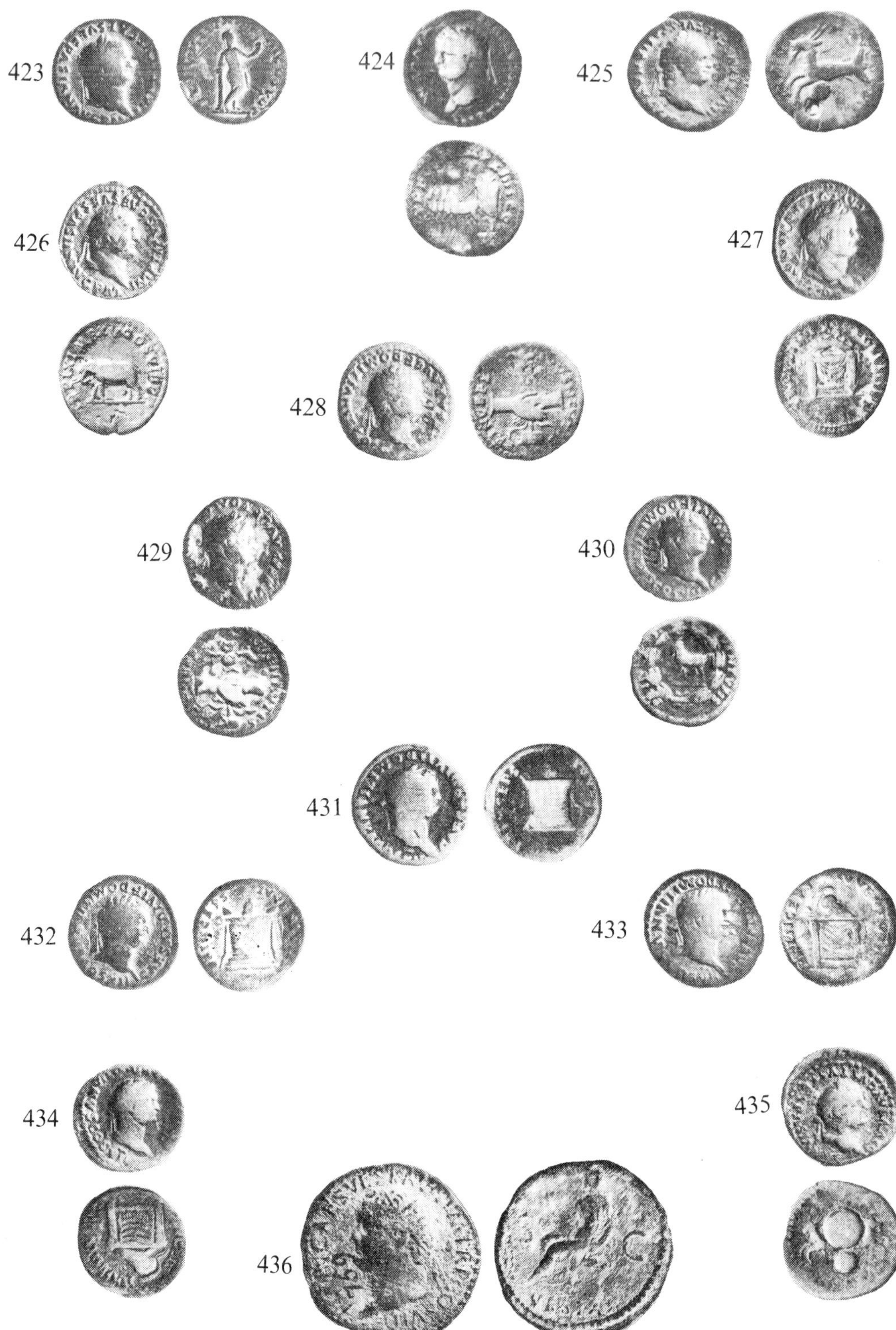
423
424
425
426
427
428
429
430
431
432
433
434
435
436

437
438
439
440
441
442
443
444

445
446
447
448
449
450
451
452
453
454
455
456
457
458
459

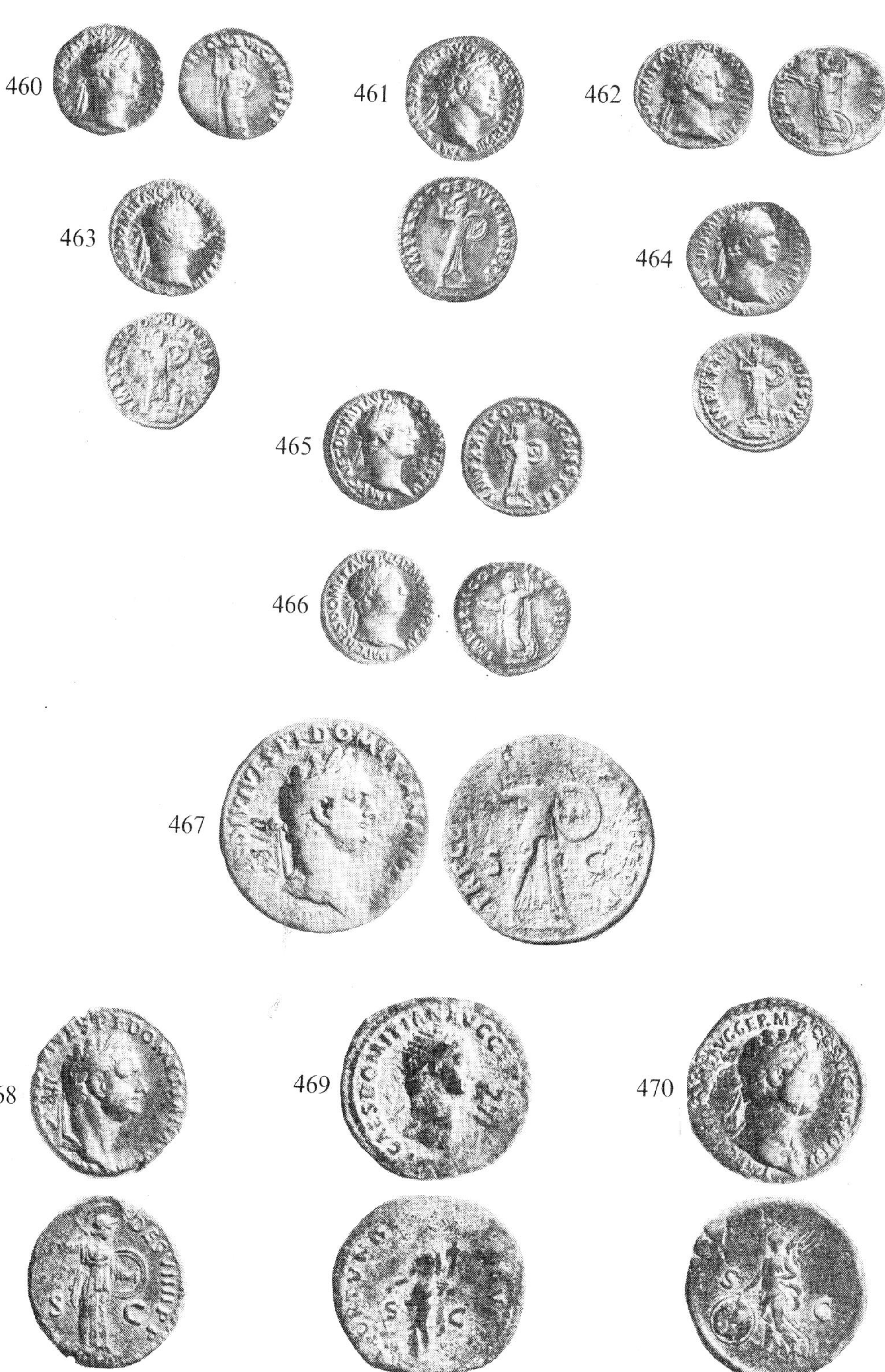
460
461
462
463
464
465
466
467
468
469
470

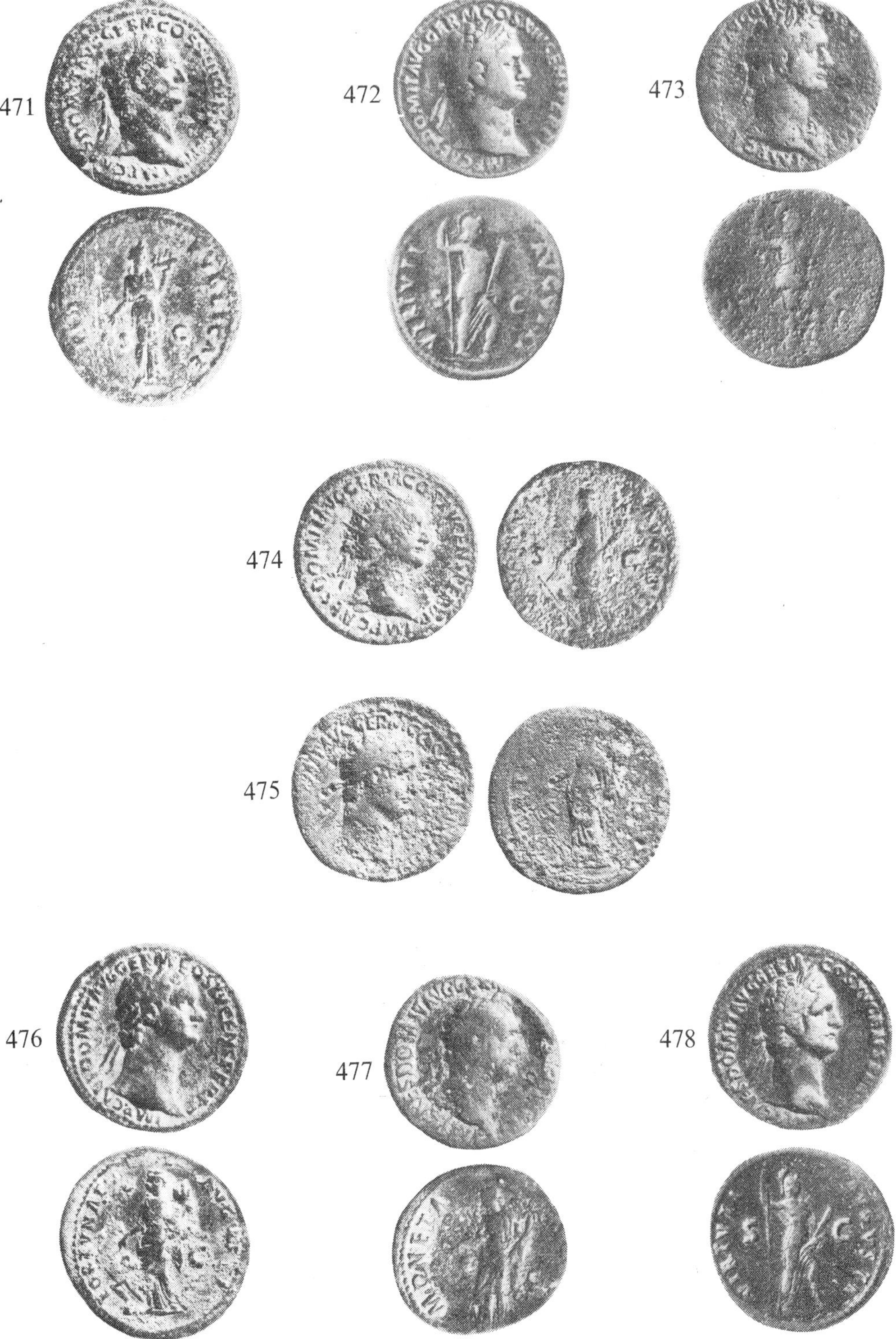
471
472
473
474
475
476
477
478

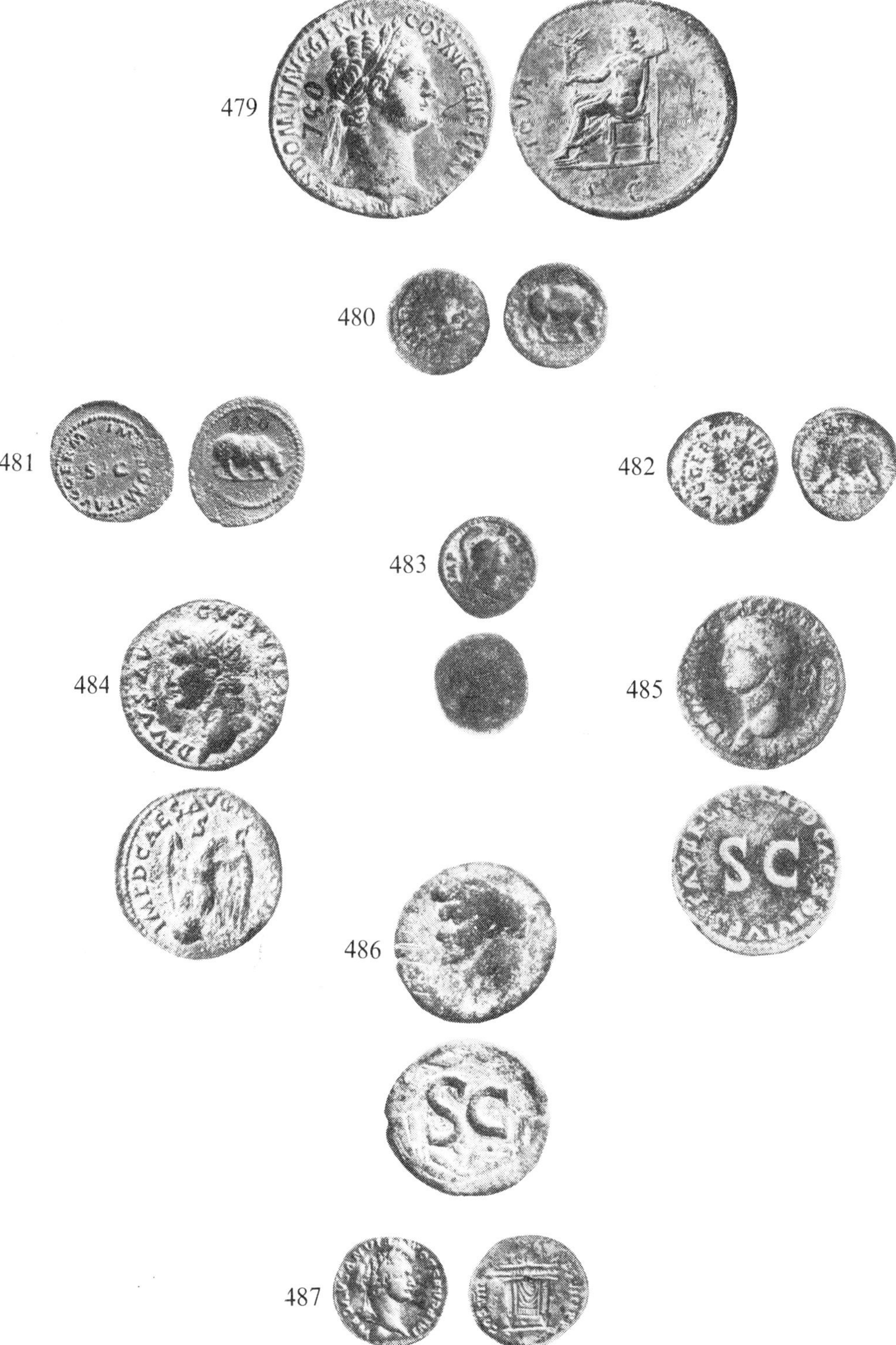
479
480
481
482
483
484
485
486
487

488
489
490
491
492
493